Microsoft Office 365 for Beginners

The 1# Crash Course From Beginners to Advanced. Easy Way to Master The Whole Suite in no Time | Excel, Word, PowerPoint, Outlook, OneNote, OneDrive, Access and Teams

GET YOUR EXCEL 2022 FREE COPY!!

Do you want to receive a free copy of my best seller Excel 2022?

Well, scan this QR CODE and download it for FREE!

Book 1 - UNDERSTANDING OFFICE 365

Introduction

You have probably heard of Office 365, which is now known as either Microsoft 365 or either of the two, but you may not understand what it is all about. Individuals' potential for productivity boost is one of Microsoft 365's primary goals. It is a subscription service that provides users with access to the most recent versions of Microsoft's contemporary productivity products that are currently on the market. It provides a wide variety of plans that can be utilized for domestic and individual purposes, as well as for businesses of all sizes, large enterprises, academic facilities, and organizations that are not for profit. Word, PowerPoint, and Excel are just some of the powerful desktop applications that are included in the Microsoft 365 plans that are designed for home and personal use. These plans, in addition to other features, also include the Microsoft Office suite. You will also have access to cloud-connected tools that enable real-time collaboration on documents and other related files, in addition to the additional online storage space that is provided. If you have a subscription, you will always have access to the most recent features, fixes, and updates to the system's security. In addition, you will receive unlimited technical support at no additional cost. When it comes to paying for your membership service, you have the choice between making payments on a monthly or annual basis. The Microsoft 365 plans for businesses, schools, and non-profit organizations all include fully installed desktop applications, which sets them apart from other cloud computing services. However, Microsoft also provides access to online versions of Microsoft Office, as well as cloud-based file storage and email services through its more fundamental subscription packages. You decide what will work best for you, regardless of whether you need it for your own small business, an enterprise, a school, or an organization that does not seek financial gain.

Chapter 1: Setting up Microsoft 365 on a Windows Device

Confirm that the requirements for office installation can be met by the device you are using, which is running the Windows operating system, and then proceed with the steps outlined below:

1.1 Go to the Online Portal at www.microsoft365.com/setup

Install Microsoft Office 365 by going to microsoft365.com/setup on your web browser while using your windows computer and then following the on-screen instructions (Edge, Firefox, Chrome, the default browser, or any other). After that, you will need to press the Enter key in order to be taken to the setup page for Microsoft 365.

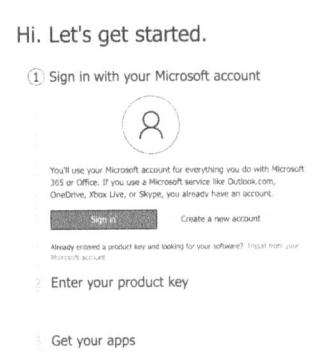

Hi. Let's get started.

1 Sign in with your Microsoft account

You'll use your Microsoft account for everything you do with Microsoft 365 or Office. If you use a Microsoft service like Outlook.com, OneDrive, Xbox Live, or Skype, you already have an account.

Sign in   Create a new account

Already entered a product key and looking for your software? Install from your Microsoft account

2 Enter your product key

3 Get your apps

1.2 Provide the Login Information for Your Microsoft Account

You are required to first sign in with your Microsoft account ID/phone number and password by clicking the 'Sign In' button on the microsoft365.com/setup website. After doing so, you will be able to finish the setup process. If this is your first time using the platform, you will need to create a new account before you can sign in. To create a new account, click the "Create Account" button, and then proceed with the steps that are listed below.

1.3 Locate the Field That Corresponds to the Product Key and Enter It There

You will see a box with instructions on how to redeem your product if you have not done so already. If this is the case, you will not see the box. In the space provided, carefully enter the 25-digit key code that you currently possess, and then click the "Submit" button. It is important to keep in mind that you cannot install Microsoft 365 straight from Microsoft if you do not already have a premium membership of some kind; you must already be subscribed to at least one of the plans.

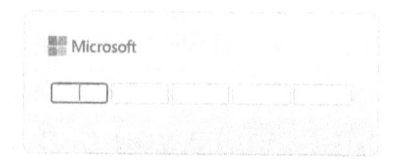

1.4 After Downloading the Microsoft 365 Installer, Install It on Your Own Computer

To get the installation process started, navigate to the following two pages and select the tabs labeled "Install" and "Install Office." You may get started with the download of Microsoft 365 by selecting one of the following choices from the menu that appears: Run, Setup, Save, or Save File, depending on the browser that is currently being used. The most recent update to Microsoft 365 will be downloaded without your intervention.

1.5 To Complete the Installation, Open the File That You Downloaded

To begin the installation process, either run the file from your browsers downloads or double-click the'microsoft365.exe' installer file that is stored in the 'Downloads' folder that is created automatically on your Windows hard drive. It will immediately start the process of installing everything.

1.6 Accept the Terms and Conditions of the Software

Because answering 'Yes' to the User Account Control question during the Office 365 software installation modifies the device configuration, it is important to do so when instructed to do so by the prompt. Following that, the software license agreement will load, at which point you must read it and then click the Accept button.

1.7 Completing the Installation in Order to Get Started

Please be patient as the installation process takes a few minutes to finish; the exact amount of time required is based on the amount of RAM available on your machine. The notification that "You're all set! The office is currently being installed and will become visible as soon as the installation is finished. Play the animated video to browse through the available apps or select the Close button to end the search process.

1.8 Finish the Installation by Activating Office 365

Any application, including Microsoft Word, must now be launched from the Windows Start Menu before it can be used. After that, you will need to agree to the terms of the license and then log in to your Microsoft account so that the process can be finished. The activation process for the Office apps is complete, and they are now available to be utilized.

Chapter 2: Essential Applications for Desktops

Microsoft 365 is a very important piece of Software. The typical consumer of the subscription package will probably not make use of all of the features that are included in the package. It is important, to get the most out of your Microsoft 365 subscription, that you are familiar with the applications that are included in the package and available for your use. At the same time, information regarding the availability of each application within the subscriptions will be provided to assist you in selecting the appropriate subscription for your needs. Within the Microsoft 365 subscription, users have access to all of the well-known desktop applications that are part of the Microsoft Office suite. Every application consists of the following:

2.1 MS Word

The word processor known as Microsoft Word may be found in the Microsoft Office 365 suite of products. Word for Windows offers support for the Portable Document Format (PDF) and OpenDocument, in addition to tools for editing and formatting documents (ODF). Word has been used as a word processing tool for a significant amount of time at this point. It is one of the company's apps that has been around the longest. Microsoft Word is one of the most widely used applications for writing documents since its user interface has undergone consistent development over the years, resulting in the addition of new capabilities and features. You have the option of starting over when you create new documents, or you can make use of one of the numerous pre-defined templates that are accessible. This tool may be used to produce a variety of documents, including business letters, resumes, product manuals, event flyers, and many more. In addition, you have the option of including a table of contents in your work, altering the header and footer, including colorized data tables and charts, and checking your work for spelling errors. Microsoft Word is a powerful program that may help your paper seem more polished and professional.

2.2 MS Excel

The remarkable history of the spreadsheet editor known as Microsoft Excel can be traced back to its conception as a competitor to the widely used Lotus 1-2-3 spreadsheet editor and its subsequent success in outselling its predecessor. This program is a Microsoft Office app that has been around for a considerable amount of time now. It is an application for spreadsheets and a strong tool that is utilized by many people across a variety of sectors. Excel is used for a variety of purposes by a wide variety of people, including accountants, teachers, project managers, and company owners. In addition to producing charts and graphs, it is also capable of doing a wide range of computations and processing data.

2.3 MS PowerPoint

The widely used program Microsoft PowerPoint is used for the creation of slides that are used in presentations. PowerPoint is often used by lecturers and instructors to illustrate their presentations since it enables viewers to get a visual representation of the information that is being sent to them.

Additionally, business professionals use PowerPoint to keep their colleagues informed on different parts of the company, and merchants utilize it to offer a presentation to the people they serve. You will also find that the built-in templates are offered to assist you in getting a smooth start with the creation of your presentation. Your presentation may considerably educate your audience by using films, music, and animation effects, all of which are enabled by PowerPoint

2.4 MS OneNote

A tool for collecting notes, Microsoft OneNote enables you to compile handwritten or typed notes, drawings, screen grabs, and audio comments into a single area. Notes may be shared with other OneNote users via the internet or a local network using OneNote, a feature that is often underutilized or not understood at all.

2.5 MS Outlook

Microsoft Outlook is a personal information manager that was first made available with the release of Office 97. It is designed to take the place of Windows Messaging, Microsoft Mail, and Schedule+. It is equipped with a calendar, an address book, a task organizer, and an email client. You may access your email account from any location in the globe by using the free web-based program known as Outlook.com, which is a web-based version of the Microsoft Outlook application.

2.6 MS OneDrive

The Microsoft OneDrive service makes it possible to sync files online and then access those files from a web browser or a mobile device using the service. This is made possible by Microsoft OneDrive. The one that comes to mind first as a potential rival is Google Drive.

2.7 MS Access

Microsoft Access is a database management system that is comprised of a comprehensive database management system formed from the combination of the relational Microsoft Jet Database Engine, a graphical user interface, and software development tools. Microsoft Access is a database management program that stores data in a format that is exclusive to the Access Jet Database Engine. Data that is saved in other applications or databases may also be imported into the application or connected directly to from inside the application itself

2.8 MS Teams

The application and service gained a lot of momentum during the COVID-19 pandemic, particularly in 2020. This was primarily because it featured one of the most useful and widely used aspects of Microsoft 365. Microsoft Teams serves as the central hub of Office 365 and is responsible for facilitating team communication, bringing members of different teams together, and providing the information and tools that are necessary for teams to be more engaged and productive. Everyone is brought closer together by the fact that they can engage at any time, whether it be by video, chat, or phone conversations. It is always possible to access documents, images, videos, the history of chat sessions, and meeting notes, which makes it much simpler to work with other individuals. The instant messaging solution that Teams provides also includes a translator, making it possible for businesses to work together regardless of the preferences and constraints they have about languages. With the help of teams, a virtual workplace can be established with all of the necessary applications, allowing workers and collaborators to remain in a single location rather than moving around from one location to another. It is frequently considered to be the workplace of the future.

Chapter 3: Choosing Your Plan

Any person or business that has elected to utilize the Microsoft 365 solution will be faced with the intriguing option of selecting which plan to use after they have decided to use the service. Because the features you receive from Microsoft 365 depend on the plan you have, certain aspects of Microsoft 365 may not be included in your subscription at all. And to tell you the truth, whether you are an individual trying to utilize it for personal in-house usage or a company looking to use it, you do not absolutely need every function that Microsoft 365 has to offer. Microsoft has additionally simplified this process by categorizing the plans into pertinent sections and, more importantly, subsections, which will assist you in making the most informed decision possible regarding what to use. As a result, a small business is not required to purchase the same plan as a larger business that may require more utilities from Microsoft 365. As a result, this ensures that everyone can choose their own plan and continue to be satisfied. In Microsoft 365, you can choose from one of four plans, each of which, of course, has its own tier of coverage:

- Microsoft 365 for Home.
- Microsoft 365 for Business.
- Microsoft 365 for Enterprise.
- Microsoft 365 for Education.

You need to look at the specifics of each plan's features and the apps that are offered to you before you can choose which one is the most suitable for your needs. It is necessary for you to be signed in to your Microsoft account to proceed with the process of subscribing to any of the Microsoft 365 plans. Keep in mind that you only need one account for everything; go ahead and establish your account and check-in.

Book 2 - MICROSOFT EXCEL 2022

Introduction

Excel has been a household name since its 1985 release. Data may be stored, sorted, and analyzed with the help of Excel, a spreadsheet tool. Microsoft's spreadsheet application is included in the company's Office 365 package. When it comes to useful features, Microsoft's Excel is up there with the best of its products. Microsoft 365 (formerly Office 365) includes the spreadsheet application Excel. The list of Excel's features and capabilities is, at first seem, inexhaustible. The capabilities of Microsoft Excel go much beyond the simple ability to create and manage databases and spreadsheets. However, it is also a "what if" computer that can do a variety of computations and calculations utilizing the data included in those cells and sheets. Let's say you've never used Microsoft Excel before or that you just want a refresher. In that scenario, you will master the fundamentals of Excel, including how to do basic arithmetic, create pivot tables, define print zones, and organize your workspace to suit your needs. Once you learn your way around the online version of Excel, you'll have no trouble working with any of your spreadsheets. Excel's online user interface is quite similar to that of the desktop version of Excel, so anybody familiar with the program should feel right at home using it.

Chapter 1: Getting Started with Spreadsheets and Templates

Templates save you time by providing an already-designed framework for your document. Making workbooks with consistent formatting is a breeze. Instead of starting with a blank workbook, you may choose from a variety of pre-made templates when you create a new document. Templates are helpful since they already have the necessary formatting and styles built in.

1.1 Utilizing Templates

The steps below will help you utilize any of these templates effectively:

- After selecting the Excel icon in the sidebar, choose "More templates" from the drop-down menu.

- As soon as the new screen loads, the highlighted section displays, which contains a list of the available templates.

- Browse the available templates and choose the one that best fits your needs.
- Input your own text instead of the sample given on the template.

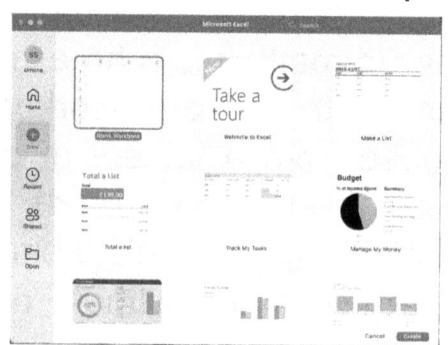

Instead of utilizing pre-made templates, try these steps to create a new page from scratch:

- After selecting the Excel icon in the sidebar, choose "New blank worksheet."
- A new, empty worksheet is now at your disposal.
- Simply go to the File menu and pick "New" to create a new workbook while you are already in the middle of working on one. To

start fresh, click the "Blank Workbook" button.

Chapter 2: Using Excel's Interface

Ribbons, groups, menus, and the spreadsheet itself make up Excel's user interface. All of these sub-components, beginning with the menus, will be examined closely.

2.1 File Title

It sits above the user interface. Every new document you make will be given a number that corresponds to a book, starting with 1. It's best to give your file a name that'll be easy to remember. In Excel, the file name may be changed by clicking the title bar. Put in the new name and choose a location to store it in Microsoft's cloud (OneDrive).

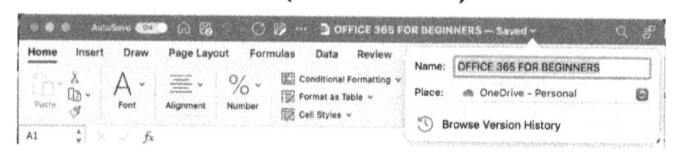

2.2 Entries on the Menus

The majority of Excel's most commonly used functions are accessible through the worksheet menus. They may be accessed from the menu bar at Excel's top. These include the standard options of File, Home, Insert, Page Layout, Formulas, Data, Review, View, and Help. You may create shortcuts by pressing the Alt key in combination with the letters that appear when you hit the Alt key. The shortcuts and menu options for each section are shown below.

File

Open, close, save and print your files here. Pressing Alt + F (on Windows) on the keyboard will bring up the find bar.

Home

From here, you may make changes to your worksheets, including formatting, editing, cutting, copying, clearing, and choosing. The quick key combination is Alt + H (on Windows).

Insert

Functions, images, tables, charts, shapes, symbols, etc. may all be included in spreadsheets here using the Insert tab. In order to use this function quickly, press Alt + N on your keyboard. (on Windows)

Page Layout

To prepare a page, go to the "Page Layout" tab. Paper size, paper orientation, printing, and scaling options are all accessible here. To print using the keyboard, use Alt + P (on Windows).

Formulas

For mathematical formulas, use Alt + M (on Windows).

Data

Here, you may organize your data and make a variety of different choices on the spreadsheets. Alt + A(on Windows) is the shortcut for this on the keyboard.

Review

This section is where you go back and double-check your previous work. You have the option of using the workbooks spellcheck and statistics features. The quick key combination is Alt + R (on Windows).

View

Workspace headers and footers, as well as the ability to see other sheets, are all accessible through the View tab. The quick cut on the keyboard is Alt + E (on Windows).

Help

Excel support is available here. You may get in touch with Excel's official support team, provide comments, search for keyboard shortcuts, and download the most recent version of Excel. A quick way to do this using just the keyboard is to press Alt + E (on Windows).

Even more, when you enter things like charts, forms, photos, and more, certain secret bars appear.

Search Box

The "Search" and "Editing/Viewing" tabs may be found in the top right of the screen.

Excel's "Search" box (also known as the "Tell me what you want to do" box) lets you look for anything inside the program, while the "Editing/Viewing" button toggles between the two respective viewing and editing modes. If you have editing permissions, you may make changes to your work or someone else's work in the Editing mode, while the Viewing option is for reading your file without making any changes. Cross-checking your work is best done in Viewing mode to prevent the accidental addition of erroneous numbers to your spreadsheet.

2.3 The Spreadsheet

Excel is a spreadsheet program that allows you to arrange information into rows and columns. These rows and columns, or cells, hold information in the form of a number value, formula, or string of text. Calculations, data organization, data analysis, pivot table generation, data visualization in the form of graphs and charts, and accurate statistical computation are all tasks that may be accomplished in a spreadsheet. The Excel spreadsheet may be tailored to your needs by adjusting the width of columns and the number of rows. Although Excel's popularity hasn't waned, many users prefer using Google Sheets, Microsoft OneNote, or OpenOffice.org Calc due to their variety of features and Excel's user-friendliness.

Chapter 3: Adding and Removing Texts

This is something that comes up regularly while dealing with a worksheet. Worksheets in Excel are collections of cells organized in rows and columns. To enter text, move the pointer to the desired cell, left click the cell, and then begin typing. In the table below, "School Record" is entered in cell A1, "Name" in cell A2, "Age" in cell B2, and "Sex" in column C2. A copy of the text in the cell you pick will appear in the formula bar, allowing you to make changes there as well. Mistakes in typing are unfortunately inevitable but know that you have the option to get them fixed if necessary. By selecting the cell and using the Backspace key, you may instantly remove any text or numbers entered into the selected cell. Using this method, the whole contents of the cell are deleted. However, if you double-clicked a cell and realized you had made a mistake, you could easily fix it by typing in the new information. You may also make changes by clicking the cell once, then the formula bar.

Calibri (Body)   12   A^ A^

Paste

B I U   ⊞   ⟋   A

A2   fx   Name

	A	B	C	D	E	F	G
1	School Record						
2	Name	Age	Sex				
3							
4							
5							

Chapter 4: Using Rows and Columns

Make the necessary edits to your spreadsheet to make your hard work seem presentable. The cells in the spreadsheet are arranged in rows and columns. Manually and mechanically adjusting the width of the rows and height of the columns to fit your data, as well as deleting them, if necessary, are also options. The varying size of the cells to Accommodate text. When your text is too long to fit in a single cell, it will seem to overlap but really remain inside the same cell. Below, cells A1 and B2 are adjacent and overlap. However, you may need to modify the column or row width so that the content appears appropriately. Allowing Excel to automatically decide how to alter the cell size to match the data is the simplest method. And they call it in Excel Autofit.

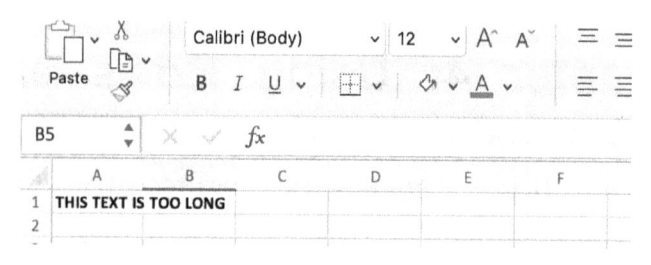

This works for both the Row Height and Column Width settings. Hovering the mouse over the row boundaries will automatically scale the row to suit the content. To do a double click, your mouse will transform into an icon, like two arrows. Your text will be formatted mechanically to suit the row width. When you need to fit a lot of text into a single cell, this feature comes in handy. Put your cursor towards the boundary of the column letters, and the column will immediately adjust to suit your screen. To do a double click, your mouse will transform into an icon, like two arrows.

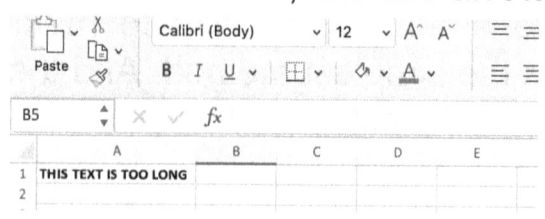

Your text will adjust itself to suit the column. When you need to fit a lot of text into a cell, this function comes in handy. The Home tab also has the option to auto-fit rows and columns. To accomplish this, just click the Home tab and then the column(s) or row(s) of interest. Select Format from the Cells submenu, and then either AutoFit Row Height or AutoFit Column Width from the drop-down menu that appears.

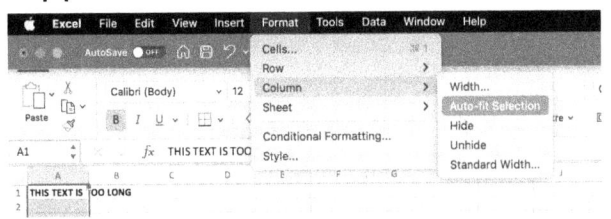

4.1 Inserting New Tables, Columns, and Rows

Including a new row requires the following steps:

- To insert a new row, choose the desired position with a right-click.
- Click the "Insert" button.

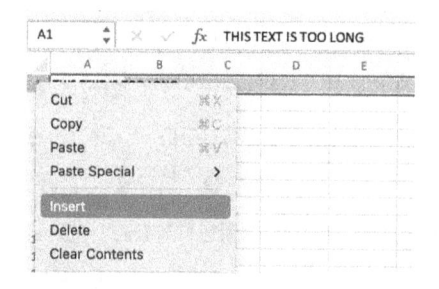

If you want to include a new column:

- To add a new column, right-click the letter of the column you wish to expand.
- Select "Insert" to begin adding columns.

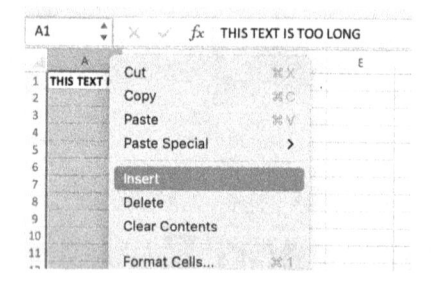

4.2 Row and Column Deletion

If you remove a row or a column, everything in that row or column will also be erased. If you just need to remove some of the information from a row or column, you may do so by removing that cell.

To get rid of a row

- To remove a row, select it and then right-click on it.
- Select "Delete" from the drop-down menu.

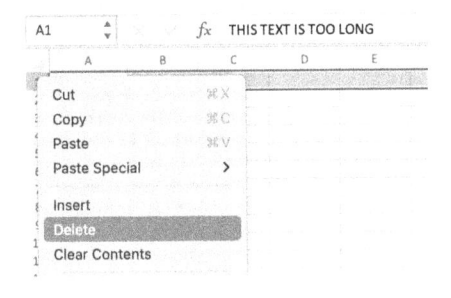

To get rid of a column

- To remove a column letter, right-click on it and choose "Delete."
- Select "Delete" from the menu.

	A1		$\times$ $\checkmark$	fx	THIS TEXT IS TOO LONG	

			D	E
1	THIS	Cut	⌘X		
2		Copy	⌘C		
3		Paste	⌘V		
4		Paste Special	>		
5					
6		Insert			
7		Delete			
8					
9		Clear Contents			
10					
11		Format Cells...	⌘1		

Chapter 5: Editing and Formatting Texts

Editing

The information that you have previously entered into a cell may be edited in one of two ways: either by hovering the cursor over the position of the cell and choosing it or by making use of the formula bar. During the course of your work, you may have observed that the formula bar updates itself following the text that you input. To modify the data that is included in the cell, either use the formula bar or use the "F2" key (on Windows) to activate the cell, which will then allow you to edit the data.

Formatting

Because the content of each cell in your work utilizes the same layout by default, it might be difficult to understand a worksheet that has an excessive amount of information because of the formatting. Your work will have that particular extra appeal by using basic formatting, which is also effective for the sake of modification. Because of this, the subject of your work is going to be easier for others to comprehend. The following is a list of formatting tools that you may use to give your work a more presentable appearance:

- Fonts
- Text Centering and Alignment
- The cell boundaries as well as the fill colors
- A painter who works in formats
- Cell styles
- Employing Bold, Italics, and Underline

Those who are acquainted with Microsoft Word are aware that making use of the bold, italic, and underline formatting options is a relatively straightforward procedure that results in your work seeming to be well-formed. If you take a glance at the Home ribbon, you will see that there are symbols for B, I, and U. The letters B, I, and U denote the use of bold, italic, and underline, respectively. To make changes to the text in a cell using B, I, or U, first select the cell or cells that contain the text you want to modify and then click any of the three icons. The effect will be applied to the text without any intervention from the user. Alterations to the chosen cell may also be made by the use of keyboard shortcuts such **as CTRL + B or Command + B for bold, CTRL + I or Command + I for italics, and CTRL + U or Command + U for underline (s).**

5.1 Using the Merge and Center Operations

Sometimes combining many cells into one might be helpful; this is particularly true if you need to include a heading in your worksheet to illustrate something properly. After doing so, numerous cells in a row will be combined into a single cell, into which you may then enter your text. On the Home tab of the ribbons are the choices to Merge and Center. There are other methods to merge cells; selecting "Merge and Center" will combine the cells you've selected and center your text, while selecting "Merge and Across" will merely combine the cells you've selected without affecting the alignment in any way. To separate cells that have been merged together, utilize the "Unmerge Cells" option. To combine cells, first, highlight the cells you wish to merge, and then choose the 'Merge and Center' option from the drop-down menu that appears. The heading that I want for my worksheet is going to be "Weekly Sales," as seen in the picture below. After you have clicked the "Merge and Center" button, it will cause the cells that have been highlighted to merge automatically, and the data will be housed in the new cell that has been generated as a result of the merging. You may be interested in styling your new heading, so go ahead and apply Bold, Italics, and Underline as you see fit. You can also adjust the font type and size as you see appropriate. Before you combine, please check to see that all of your data is present in the first cell since any information that is wiped out during the merging process can never be retrieved again. Despite this, you can reverse your activities up to the point when you save and shut your document. To unmerge cells that have been merged for any reason, click the cell that has been merged, then click the arrow that is located next to the words "Merge and Center" on the Home ribbon, and choose "Unmerge Cells."

5.2 Data Alignment

Aligning your data implies structuring your data. You have the option of arranging the data that is included inside your cells and keeping it to the left, right, center or justifying it. You may also arrange things to be on top, in the center, or at the bottom. Alternately, you may make the indentation deeper or shallower. On the other hand, you'll find each of them on the Home tab on the ribbon. If you have more than one cell that has to be aligned, choose the cell or cells that you want to align first. After that, decide whether you want to align the left, center, or right. The data are now aligned to the left in the example that may be seen below. Use the other alignment types for your purposes to have a better understanding of how each one operates.

Chapter 6: Charts, Functions and Formulas

6.1 Charts

When looking for patterns in a collection of information or data that is laid out in columns and rows, we often utilize charts.

6.2 Different Kinds of Charts

The following is a list of the many kinds of charts and the applications for each one:

Pie Chart

You may demonstrate and quantify a numerical comparison of elements with the use of pie charts, which are available for usage. The data in this style of the chart is shown in a circular format and, more often than not, in percentage form.

Bar charts

Such charts are a form of a chart that may be used to show values and compare those values to one another. The comparison is carried out using categories, and the values are most often shown in the form of rectangular bars whose lengths are in direct proportion to the values they represent.

Column charts

These are useful tools for displaying and quantifying the

numerical comparison of a variety of different elements. In order to better show the data being displayed, this chart makes use of vertical rectangular bars.

Line Charts

Another name for this kind of graph is a line graph. This chart may be used to compare more than one piece of data by constituting more than one line, or it can be used to compare a single set of data to another.

Combo Charts

This chart takes data from many categories and combines them into a single visual representation. It is referred to as a combination chart; hence, you may refer to it as a "combo" for short. It is used to combine the qualities of the bar chart with the properties of the line chart.

6.3 Building a Chart

To create a chart, one must:

- Determine and choose the information or data that will serve as the basis for the chart that will be prepared for you.
- Select a chart from the Insert tab's drop-down menu.
- You may choose any of the suggested charts by scrolling through the list of them and clicking on them. See what your data looks like.

6.4 Formulas

Excel is pre-loaded with its own unique formulas for resolving a variety of issues, similar to the straightforward mathematical formulas that were available to you when you were still in elementary school and were used to solve problems. Expressions are the form that these formulas take, and they operate on the values that are contained within a cell. The four fundamental operations of mathematics that may be performed in Excel are addition, subtraction, division, and multiplication. Excel makes it easy to add numbers; all you need to do is enter the "=" symbol, the numbers, and the "+" sign in between them, and then press the Enter key. The total is shown in the corresponding cell. You may also add the values of the cells by simply putting the equal sign ("="), the cell names, and then the plus sign ("+") to separate them. After that, the result of adding up the values contained in each cell is shown when you hit the "Enter" button on your keyboard.

6.5 Functions

Excel functions are formulae that have already had their complexity reduced to a manageable level. When making use of a function, the function itself must be entered into the cell in which the desired result is to be shown. You may, for example, decide to calculate the total of a column in your worksheet. The SUM function has been added to the very last cell (G10), and the formula reads as follows: =SUM(G3:G9). This represents the total value of the cells G3, G4, G5,..., and G9. After that, you must validate the function by pressing the "Enter" button. This approach may be used for a variety of tasks. The following is a list of fundamental features that you may include in your Excel workflow:

SUM

=SUM(firstcellname:lastcellname)

AVERAGE

=AVERAGE(firstcellname:lastcellname)

IF

=IF(logical test, value if true, value if false)

SUMIFS

=SUMIFS(sum range, criteria range 1, criteria 1, …)

COUNTIFS

=*COUNTIFS(criteria range 1, criteria 1, …)*

TRIM

=TRIM(text)

CONCATENATE

=CONCATENATE(text 1, text 2, text 3, …,)

VLOOKUP

=VLOOKUP(lookup value, table array, column index number, range lookup)

Chapter 7: Saving and Printing Your Document

7.1 Saving Your Documents

While you are working on a paper, you may find that you need a break from time to time, regardless of whether or not the job is finished. You have the option of saving your papers either while you are working on them or after you have finished working on them. The first option is the one that is often used if there is a need to save one's current progress to return to a task at a later time. Despite this, you should be aware that your document will be saved without your intervention at regular intervals. The sole option available to you is to save as; doing so will allow you to save your document in a particular folder on OneDrive. The following are some of the things that may be done to preserve your work:

- In the upper left corner of your screen, you'll see a tab labeled

"File." Move your pointer to that tab.

- You will be presented with a selection of choices after you open the menu.
- Pick a file type to save it as.
- You will see a window that allows you to choose the location where you would want your document to be stored.
- Simply clicking the Save button will save your work.

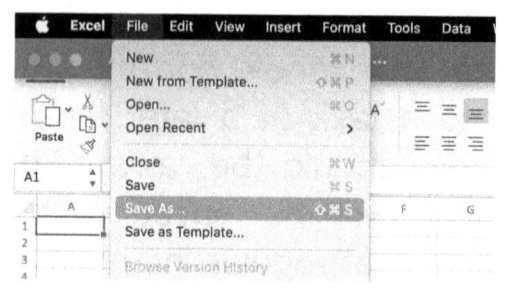

7.2 Printing Your Document

When everything is finished and ready, you can decide that you want a tangible copy of your paper, which you can do by printing it off. Follow the steps outlined below:

- To print the document, go to the "File" menu and pick "Print."

- You will see a dialogue window that provides you with the opportunity to preview your document.
- After selecting the desired quantity of copies to print, click the "print" button.

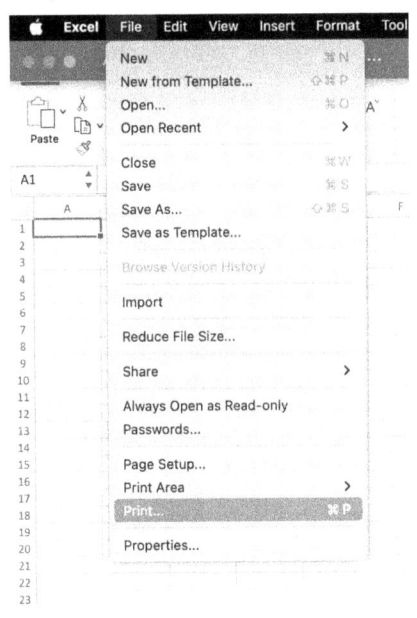

Book 3 - MICROSOFT WORD 2022

Introduction

One of the most well-known tools produced by Microsoft is Word. Word is used in many different settings, including educational institutions, business environments, administrative workplaces, and many more. In most cases, the traditional version of Microsoft Word may be accessed on Windows 10 by selecting the "Start" menu, finding the "Word" application in the list of available programs, and clicking on the "Open" button. This book will teach you keyboard shortcuts and other instructions that will make you a more efficient user of Microsoft Word 365. Everything in this book was written with one goal in mind: to let you leave work sooner and go home through a more leisurely, picturesque route. From this point on, you will learn how to build new document views and modify existing ones. You get familiar with the skills necessary to mark your position in lengthy documents, pick text, and navigate between locations. You will also learn how to insert one document into another, how to have Word read aloud to you, and how to design data-entry forms to make it simpler to submit information.

Chapter 1: Document Creation and Template Usage

The first and foremost step we would require before starting to use Word 365 is accessing or downloading it on your system. Without having access to Word 365, your options and features would be limited to 'View-Only'. The editing option would be unlocked only after your program is successfully installed and signed in using your Microsoft Credentials.

1.1 Getting Access to Word 365

Since it can be accessed via the internet, Office 365 Word is distinct from the traditional version of Microsoft Word that is installed on both Windows and Mac computers. You have access to the online application if you are using a web browser, which should already be installed on your computer. This will allow you to complete this task properly. Simply sign into your Office 365 account and choose the Word icon located on the sidebar to have access to the program. After that, a website will load up for you that has a few different choices to help you get started. You may create a new document by clicking on "New blank document," choose a template to use or get more templates by clicking on "More templates," upload previous documents for editing by clicking on "Upload and open," and access recently used, pinned, and shared files from this section.

1.2   Template Option

Templates provide you with a framework and layout that has already been set, which helps you save a lot of time. It makes it possible for you to create papers that use comparable formatting standards with no effort on your part. When you make a new document, rather than starting with a sheet of blank fresh paper, you have the option of choosing whatever template you want to use instead. The use of templates is beneficial since they already have all of the necessary styles and formatting included in them. In order to make use of a template of your choosing, please follow the steps below:

- After clicking on the Word symbol in the sidebar, choose "More templates" from the drop-down menu that appears.
- The highlighted section of the new screen comes up and displays a list of templates.
- You may go through all of the available templates and choose one that best fits the needs of your project.

- Simply insert your own text instead of the one that is shown on the template.

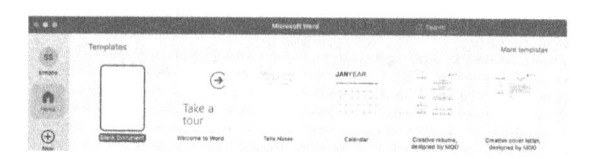

1.3   Inserting Blank Page

Instead of utilizing templates, you may construct a blank page by following the methods that are outlined below:

- After clicking on the Word icon in the sidebar, go to the "File" menu and choose "New Blank Document."
- You should now be looking at a blank page.

In addition, if you are currently working on a document and you want to create a new document, all you have to do is click the File menu and pick "New" from the drop-down menu that appears. After that, choose "New blank document" from the menu.

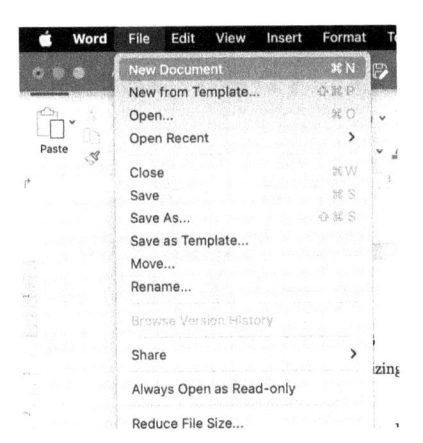

Chapter 2: The Interface of the Word

The user interface of the web-based version of Word is quite similar to that of the traditional edition of Microsoft Word. The most significant distinction is that to use the online version, you need to have a web browser and an active internet connection. The menus, ribbons, groups, and the actual document page are the components that make up the Word interface. Beginning with the menus, we are going to go into each of these distinct components in its own right.

2.1 The Document Title

This may be found in the upper left-hand corner of the user interface. When you create a new file, Windows will give it the default name Document 1, followed by Document 2, Document 3, and so on. Changing the name of your file so that it is more user-friendly is, however, strongly recommended. Simply click the title button, which is located at the very top of the Word interface, to make changes to the name of your file. Enter the new name, and then pick the location on the Microsoft Cloud where you would want the file to be stored (OneDrive).

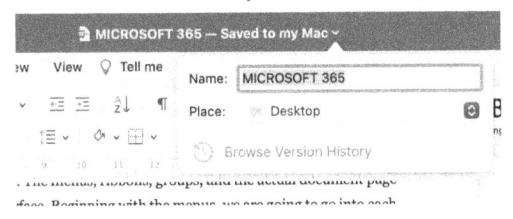

2.2 Various Menus

The majority of the commands that you will regularly use in Word are located inside the various menus. They may be found at the very top of the user interface for Word. They are labeled as the "File," "Home," "Insert," "Layout," "References," "Review," and "View" menu options, respectively. The many capabilities of each menu are detailed below.

File

This is the section of the program where you may carry out tasks such as opening, closing, saving, and printing files.

Home

This is the location from which you carry out tasks, including formatting, editing, cutting, copying, clearing, and choosing from the pages of your document.

Insert

This is the section of the document page where you may do operations such as inserting page breaks, photos, tables, header & footer, page numbers, symbols, and so on.

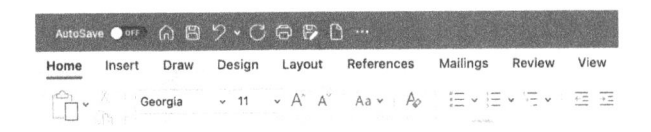

Page Layout

It is where you will conduct the page configuration for the document. In this section, you will find options to adjust the size of your paper, the orientation of your paper, the margins, the indentation, and the spacing.

References

This enables you to add tables of contents and footnotes to the manuscript you are working on.

Review

At this point, you should double-check everything that you have accomplished up to this point.

View

This feature gives you the ability to view your papers in a variety of formats. In this menu, you also have the option to zoom in on your document.

Help

If you need assistance with Word, go no further than here. You have the option of directly contacting Word support, sending comments, searching for keyboard shortcuts, and looking for the most recent update to Word

2.3 The Ribbon Area

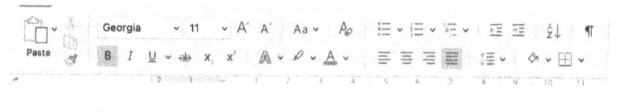

This is the top area on the page for the document, and it may be found just below the menus. After you have created or opened a document, the Home menu will be chosen by default, which will cause the Home ribbon to be shown. Tabs and icons that are essential to the completion of all Word-related operations may be found on the ribbon. There are command buttons, groups, tabs, and launchers for dialogues, and all are included inside the ribbon. You may find that the current appearance of your ribbon is not to your liking; to alter the style of your ribbon, click the little arrow symbol that is located in the top right corner.

Chapter 3: Entering and Deleting Texts

3.1 The Process of Entering Text

You will now begin to make changes to and develop the document that you have previously generated when you reach this stage. You'll see that the Word program's user interface has a blank area in the shape of a rectangle. To begin typing in your document, move the pointer to the empty area, and then click the left button on your mouse.

Page Layout

Utilizing the Page Layout option will allow you to clean up, organize, and attractively present your work. To do this, just choose the Page Layout option and make any adjustments that are required or advised.

Margins

They are a useful tool that will assist you in creating empty spaces at the top, bottom, left, and right sides of your page.

Orientation

Regarding the document's orientation, you have the option of selecting either the portrait or the landscape view.

Size

By default, your page size is Letter (8.5" x 11" / 21,59 cm x 27,94 cm). Nevertheless, you have the option of picking a different size or configuring a custom size if you already have one.

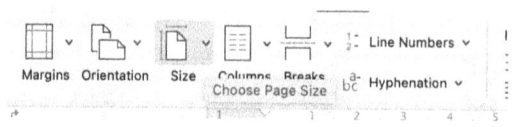

3.2 Deleting Texts

You may make some mistakes when you type the text into your document, and you'll probably want to fix any mistakes. Follow these steps:

If you want to erase a set of words, you have two options: either move your mouse to those words and keep clicking on the "backspace" key on your keyboard, or you may click and hold and then drag over those words to highlight them. Both of these options will do the same thing. Then, to erase, use the "backspace" key on your keyboard.

Chapter 4 - Editing and Formatting Text

When you edit and format text in Word, you are editing and changing the look of the text to make a better document. This is done for a variety of reasons. You may easily alter or format text by doing the following right:

- Selecting the text that will be formatted will be your first step. You may choose a single word by double click on it to make your selection.
- You may pick numerous words at once by clicking and holding on to the words you want to select and then dragging your mouse over the words that you want to select.
- Select the method of formatting that best suits your needs. It might be to alter the typeface, the color of the font, the size of the font, or even to make the text italicized, bold, or underlined.

4.1 The Font Size, Style and Color

It is possible to generate a document that is useful and well-organized by modifying the typeface, the size of the font, and the color of the font in some different ways.

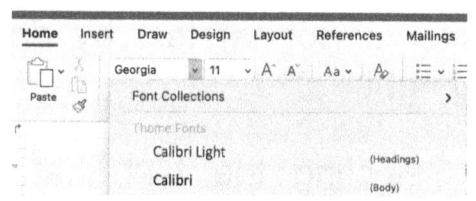

- To alter the font of your text:
- Choose the text for which you want to make adjustments or alter the font.
- To access the font drop-down menu, move your cursor to the Home tab and then click on the arrow that is located next to the font name.
- When you place the cursor over each font, you will get a preview of that font in the text that is now chosen.
- When you make your selection, the document will automatically update to reflect the new font,

replacing the one it previously had.

- Altering the size of a Font is accomplished by:
- Mark the text you want to modify to adjust its font size, and then highlight it.
- Move your mouse cursor to the Home section, and then touch on the downward pointer that's beside the size box. This will display a drop-down menu with a variety of number options.
- You may choose the size of the font you wish to use, and the change will be reflected in the text that you have picked. You may also use your keyboard to enter the number you want to dial and then hit the Enter key on your keyboard.
- You also have the option of making your font larger or smaller by selecting either the substantial capital letter A or the little capital letter A located at the very top of the page.

To make a change to the color of a font

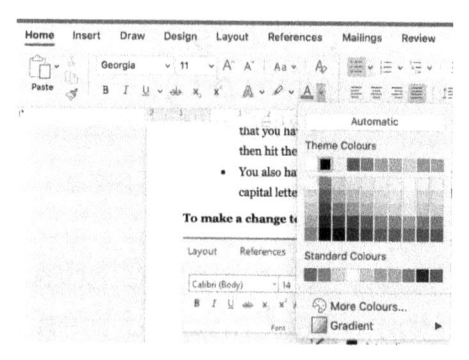

- Select the text for which you wish the color to be changed.
- You may access a drop-down menu by selecting the arrow that is located next to the Font Color on the Home tab.
- If you move the mouse cursor over some different font colors, you will get a preview of them applied to the text that is now chosen.
- You may also launch a dialogue box containing colors by clicking on "More Colours," which is located at the bottom of the list. Choose the one that appeals to you the most, then click the OK

button, and the color of the text you have picked will change.

- In addition, you may alter the color that is used to highlight text by going to the Home tab, clicking on the arrow that is located next to the Text Highlight Colour option, and then selecting a color from the resulting drop-down menu.

4.2 Underlining, Bolding, and Italicizing

You have the option in Word to format your text using bold, italics, or underlining. To accomplish any of these goals: Mark the words you wish to change by highlighting them.

You may make the text you have highlighted bold by going to the Home area, tapping the letter B, which stands for the bold button, or by using your keyboard to hit the CTRL/Command combination. You can make the words italic by either clicking on the letter I that is represented by the italic button on the tab or by pressing the Ctrl/Command + I keys on your keyboard. If you go back to the Home tab and either click on the letter U or press the Ctrl/Command key together with the letter U on your keyboard, the text that you have chosen will be highlighted.

4.3 Number and Bullet List

When creating a list in Word, you have the choice of using either numbered or bulleted format. Both of these things make it easier for readers to grasp the steps. While tutors often use bulleted lists to highlight the most important aspects of their courses for their students, In manuals, step-by-step instructions are often presented in the form of numbered lists for the convenience of the reader.

- To create a numbered or bulleted list in the formatting toolbar, click the appropriate button.
- To begin, press the numbers button, followed by the dot key (which looks like a 1), and then press the spacebar.
- After entering the first item on the list, press the Enter key.
- When you go to the next line, the number will automatically continue where it left off on the previous line.
- Enter the following item, and then hit the Enter key.
- When you are completed with the process of listing or bulleting items, hit the Enter key twice to terminate the operation.
- If you move the cursor to the right of the number or the bullet and then press the backspace key, you will be able to delete the list or bullet.
- If you want to convert a numbered list into a bulleted list, select the entire list, then go to the Home tab of the Paragraph

group and click on the icon that looks like a bullet.

In addition to the default ones that you have seen, you can also examine the available number and bullet listing by checking the number and bullet dialogue box. This will allow you to see all of the numbers and bullets that are currently accessible. After making your selection, all you have to do is hit the "Okay" button to include it in your work.

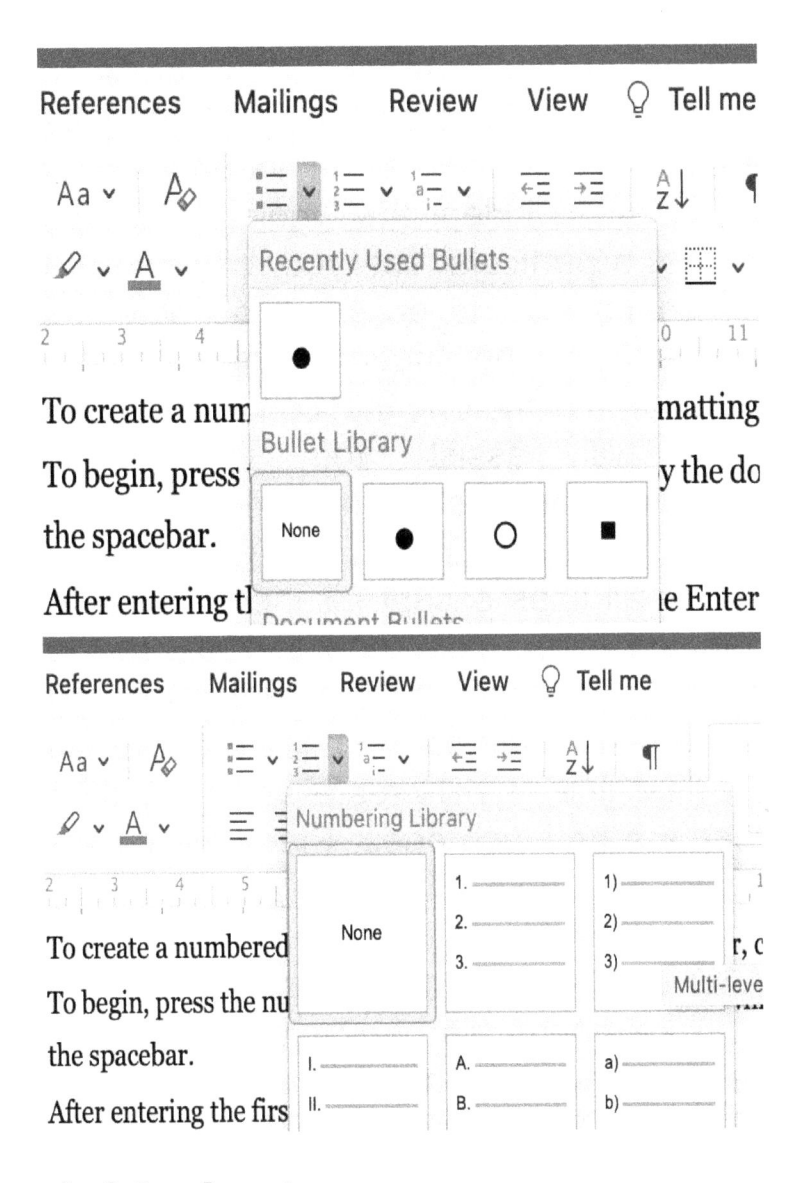

4.4 Indents

Adding structure to important parts of your page may be accomplished quite effectively via the use of indentation. If you wish to indent the whole paragraph or just a particular list, you may use the horizontal ruler to do this. The only line that has to be indented before each paragraph is the one that comes before it. This will assist you in visually distinguishing each part from the others in the document. You may also choose to indent all lines except for the first line. A hanging indent is a term that is used to describe this action. Utilizing the Tab key is a speedy method for indenting text. On the first line, it will create an indentation that is a half inch deep. Place the cursor where you want it to be at the beginning of each section that you want to indent. After that, you need to hit the Tab key on your keyboard. The text on the first line will be moved to the right by a half inch when this adjustment is made.

In addition, you may adjust the amount of space between lines of text in a paragraph by highlighting the text and then clicking the increase or decrease indent button located in the Home tab's Paragraph group. This will apply the change to all of the text in the paragraph. Each line of the paragraph would be indented to the left or right, depending on which style was being used.

4.5 Developing a Table of Contents

When working on a substantial project, it might be challenging to recall the information that is presented on the pages. On the other hand, Microsoft Word enables you to include a table of contents in your document, which makes the process of organizing it brisk and uncomplicated. The following are the stages:

- When you use a heading style that is found on the Home tab under the Styles group as titles in your document, it shows that you have established a new section of your document. If you want to learn more about how to achieve this, check out the next section. In addition, the addition of a table of contents should not be too difficult.

- After the heading style has been set, it will just take a few clicks for you to input the content of your table. After selecting the References tab, go to the Table of Contents group and choose the icon labeled "Table of Contents" from inside that group. The table of contents will then appear in your project when you make your selection from the drop-down menu that appears next to the box containing the pre-installed tables.

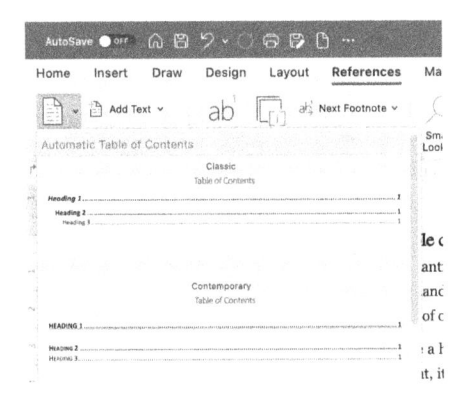

- Whether you want to change your document or add to it, bringing the table of contents up to date is a breeze. Click the Update Field button after you have the table of contents highlighted. Choose the option to Update the Entire Table once the corresponding dialogue box appears.
- When the update is complete, the table of contents will highlight any changes that have been made to the document.

Cut   ⌘ X
Copy   ⌘ C
Paste   ⌘ V

Reply to Comment
Delete Comment
Resolve Comment

Update Field   ⌥⇧⌘ U
Toggle Field Codes

Font...   ⌘ D
Paragraph...   ⌃⌘ M

New Comment

iPhone or Simone
Take Photo
Scan Documents
Add Sketch

Chapter 5: Inserting In Word

In most cases, Microsoft Word is the application of choice for the production of a variety of documents. In the end, the kind of written work you want to produce is the primary factor in determining the components that you put into your paper.

Inserting tables into documents is necessary to fulfill the requirements for the tabular representation of data (such as results, rankings, and charts, amongst other things). The same logic applies to papers that need a graphical representation; in which case you will need to incorporate relevant images. It is common to practice utilizing the "Insert" tab in Microsoft Word to accomplish the task of inserting new elements into existing word documents. The following is a list of things that you can include in your word document.

5.1 Tables

Follow the steps below to insert a table into your document:

- Select the "Insert" tab by clicking on it.
- To see the table, choose the "Table" option.
- Left-clicking the mouse after you have selected the required number of rows and columns to display in the table will do this. Almost immediately, the table will appear in your document.

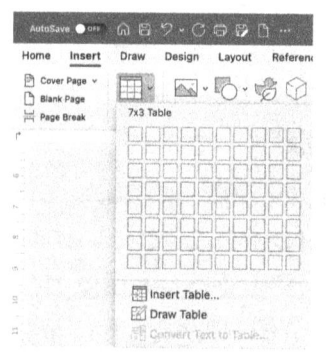

5.2 Photo

Follow the steps below to incorporate a picture or image into your document:

- Select the "Insert" tab by clicking on it.
- To see the image, use the "Picture" option.

- Please choose a place from where you would like to insert an image.

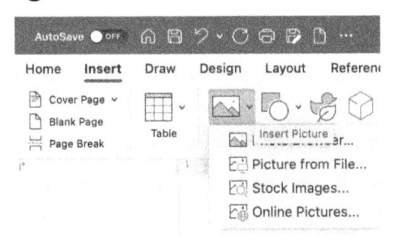

5.3 Inserting a Page Break

Follow the steps below to successfully insert a page break:

- Select "Insert" from the drop-down menu.
- To create a page break, click the "Page Break" button.

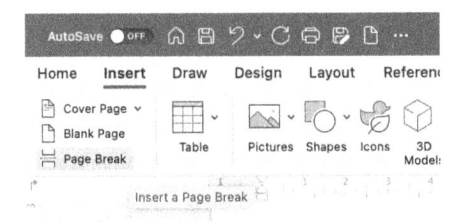

5.4 Links

The following steps need to be taken to insert a link:

- Select "Insert" from the drop-down menu.
- Select the "Link" button and click it.

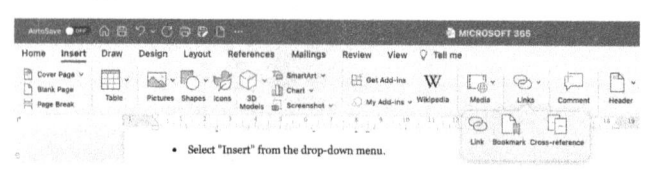

5.5 Inserting a Header or Footer

You can insert a header or footer by following the steps outlined below:

- Select "Insert" from the drop-down menu.
- Select the "Header" or "Footer" button from the menu.

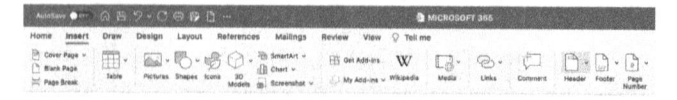

5.6 Inserting a Page Number

Follow the steps below to insert a page number:

- Select "Insert" from the drop-down menu.

- Select "Page Numbers" from the drop-down menu.
- Opt for a certain style.

Chapter 6: Saving and Printing Your Documents

6.1 Saving Documents

While you are working on a paper, you may find that you need a break from time to time, regardless of whether or not the job is finished. You have the option of saving your documents either while you are working on them or after you have finished working on them. The first option is the one that is typically chosen whenever there is a need to save one's current progress to return to a task at a later time. Despite this, you should be aware that your document will be saved without your intervention at regular intervals. The sole option available to you is to save as; doing so will allow you to save your document in a particular folder on OneDrive.

The following are some of the things that can be done to save your work:

- When you move your cursor to the "File" tab, which is located in the top-left corner of your screen, a menu with a list of available choices will be shown.

- Pick a file type to save it as.
- You will see a window that allows you to choose the location where you would want your document to be stored.
- Simply clicking the Save button will save your document.

6.2 Printing Documents

When everything is finished and ready, you can decide that you want a tangible copy of your paper, which you can do by printing it off. Follow the steps outlined below:

- To print the document, go to the "File" menu and pick "Print."
- You will see a dialogue box that provides you with the opportunity to preview your document.
- Select the number of copies that you want to be printed, and then press the button that says print.

Book 4 - MICROSOFT POWER POINT 2022

Introduction

PowerPoint provides you with all of these benefits and more thanks to its level playing field that makes it accessible to everyone who is aware of their audience. PowerPoint is a program that may be used to present data by including text, images, animation, and effects in the transitions between slides. It also gives you the ability to build an oral presentation using a collection of slides, which will help you become a better speaker. It is frequently stated that there is power in vision, and with it, you provide the ability to visualize to your audience. The Office 365 Platform PowerPoint brings together some resources that are available on the web to create presentations that are highly clear on a web browser.

Chapter 1: Getting Access to Microsoft PowerPoint 365

The Office 365 Platform PowerPoint brings together some resources that are available on the web to create presentations that are highly clear on a web browser. Simply logging into your Office 365 account and selecting the PowerPoint icon from the sidebar will get you access to the presentation software. After that, a website will load up for you that has a few different choices to help you get started. You can create a new presentation by clicking on "New blank presentation," select a template to use or obtain additional templates by clicking on "More templates," upload previous documents for editing by clicking on "Upload and open," and access recently used, pinned, and shared files from this section.

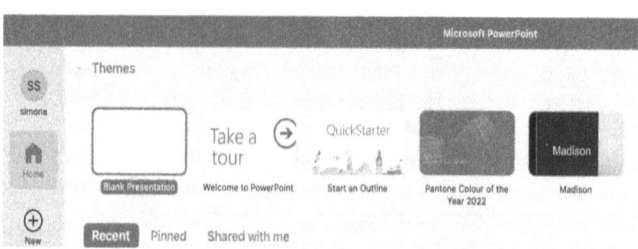

Chapter 2: Development of a New Presentation and Template Usage

The use of themes or templates provides you with a framework and layout that has already been chosen, which helps you save a lot of time. It makes it possible for you to create presentations that use comparable formatting standards with very little effort on your part. When you start a new presentation, rather than starting with a blank page like you normally would, you have the option of choosing whatever theme you want to use. One of the advantages of adopting themes is that they already have all of the necessary formatting and style information built in. You may use whatever theme you choose by adhering to the procedures listed below:

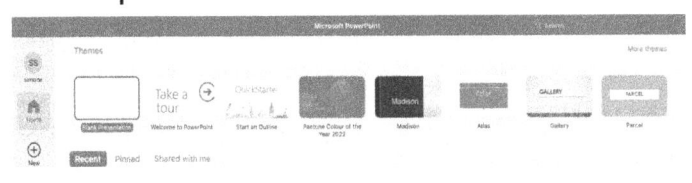

- After clicking on the PowerPoint icon in the sidebar, choose

"More themes" from the drop-down menu that appears.

- The highlighted section of the new screen comes into view and displays a list of the themes.
- You may pick any of the available themes to use for your project by scrolling through all of them.
- Replace the wording that is currently shown on the themes with your own content.

If you would rather not use themes for your presentation, you may develop one from scratch by following the steps below:

- Right after clicking on the PowerPoint icon in the sidebar, choose 'New blank presentation' from the drop-down menu that appears.
- You are currently in possession of an empty presentation.
- Simply clicking the "File" menu and selecting "New" while you are currently working on a presentation and wanting to

make a new presentation is all that is required of you when you want to do so. Next, choose "New blank presentation" from the drop-down menu.

Chapter 3: The Interface Used for PowerPoint

The interface of the web-based version of PowerPoint is quite similar to that of the traditional version of Microsoft PowerPoint. The most significant distinction is that to use the online version, you need to have a web browser and an active internet connection. The presentation page itself, in addition to the other menus, ribbons, and groups that make up the PowerPoint interface. Beginning with the menus, we are going to go into each of these distinct components in its own right.

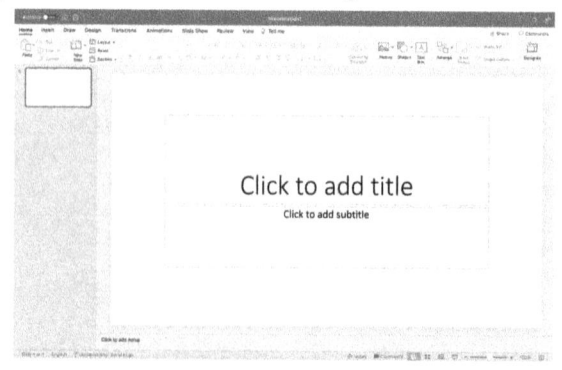

3.1 The Project Title

This may be found in the upper left-hand corner of the user interface. The names Presentation 1, Presentation 2, Presentation 3, and so on are those that are given to newly created files whenever you create a new one by default.

Changing the name of your file so that it is more user-friendly is, however, strongly recommended. Simply select the title button, which is located at the very top of the PowerPoint user interface, to make changes to the name of your file. Enter the new name, and then pick the location on the Microsoft Cloud where you would want the file to be stored (OneDrive).

3.2 Various Menus

The majority of the commands that you will regularly use in PowerPoint are located in its various menus. These options may be found at the very top of the user interface. These are the File, Home, Insert, Draw, Design, Transitions, Animations, Slide Show, Review, and View menu options, as well as the Help option. The many capabilities of each menu are detailed below.

File

This is the section of the program where you may carry out tasks such as opening, closing, saving, and printing files.

Home

This is where you execute actions like adding new slides, formatting, editing, cutting, copying, clearing, and choosing

from your Presentation slide. Home is also where you may choose from your Presentation slide.

Insert

This is where you may execute operations such as putting new slides into the presentation slide. Other operations include inserting photos, tables, shapes, icons, SmartArt, text boxes, audio, video, footer, slide numbers, and symbols, among other things.

Draw

This section provides tools that will assist you in drawing and erasing.

Design

The design incorporates some unique motifs and permutations into its finished products. In this section, you may also personalize your slides; for example, you can change the size of the slide and add either photos or solid fills to the backdrop.

Transitions

This section gives you access to a variety of slide effects that may be used in your presentation.

Animations

This also assists you in adding animation effects to the slide that you are working on.

Slide Show

Click this option when you are ready to deliver the slideshow that you have prepared. Then choose either "From Beginning" or "From Current Slide" from the drop-down menu.

3.3 Search Bar

In addition, the "Search" and "Editing/Viewing" buttons may be found in the center of the interface's top bar. You can search for anything in PowerPoint by using the "Search" box, which is also the "Tell me what you want to do" box. The "Editing" button allows you to go between the Editing mode and the Viewing mode. The Editing mode gives you the ability to make modifications to your own work as well as the work of other people, provided that you grant them the opportunity. In addition, the Viewing mode only allows you to navigate the contents of your file without making any changes to it. During the time that you are double-checking your work, it is essential to switch your presentations to the Viewing mode. This will prevent you from inadvertently adding values to your presentation that you do not want.

3.4 The Ribbon

This is the uppermost part of the presentation slide, and it may be found just behind the menus. After you have created or opened a presentation, the Home menu will be chosen by default, which will cause the Home ribbon to be shown. The Ribbon in PowerPoint is where you'll find all of the tabs and icons you'll need to complete your various duties. Tabs, command buttons, groups, and conversation launchers are some of the components that make up the Ribbon. You may find that the current appearance of your Ribbon is not to your liking. To change the appearance of your Ribbon, click on the little arrow symbol that is located in the top right corner.

Chapter 4: Designing a New Slide

When you begin with a blank presentation, you will initially just have one slide available for use as a Title and Subtitle slide. After that, you will include more materials in your presentation. In order to do this, you will need to develop more slides.

4.1 Creating a Blank Slide

To make a new slide, do the following:

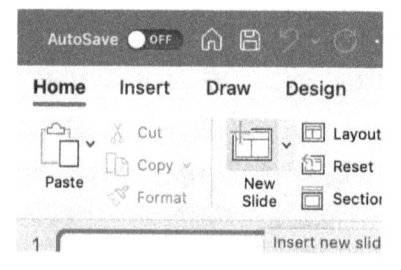

- To create a new slide, choose "New Slide" from the Home menu.
- After that, choose a format for your slide, and then click the "Add Slide" button.
- Your presentation slides will be shown in the pane that is located

on the left-hand side of the interface.

- When you create a new slide, it will often be produced below the slide that is presently chosen in the presentation.

4.2 Adding Design Theme

PowerPoint Online does not allow users to store their customized themes. However, it has its own themes, each of which comes pre-designed with a particular layout, color scheme, and font family. If you choose one of these themes, the modifications will be applied to every one of your slides. You may easily apply a theme to a presentation by picking the 'Design' tab at the beginning of the presentation and then selecting a theme from the Themes set of options that appear.

Follow these steps if you have an existing presentation and want to modify the design, theme, or color scheme:

- Navigate to the Design tab and choose a color or variation from the Group for Variants drop-down menu.

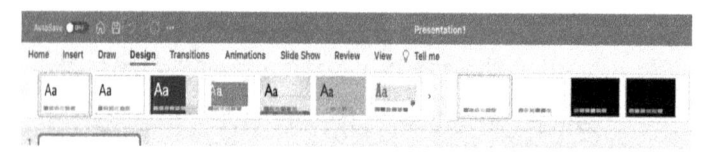

- As you create new slides, you have the option of applying a variety of various styles to those slides by choosing the Designer icon located on the Home page. After that, a navigation window featuring several styles will appear on the right-hand side of your screen.
- As you create a new slide, choose a presentation format for it from the navigation pane.

Chapter 5: Entering and Formatting Text

PowerPoint is often regarded as one of the most efficient presentation formats. Words have to be included in the information you provide, and those words have to be interesting and helpful to the people reading them. After developing your presentation, the next step is to add some sentences to provide it with some context.

5.1 Text Addition

Your presentation will begin with the first slide, including two text boxes that are, by default, designed for the presentation subject and the creator of the presentation. To add text to the text boxes, click within the box and then input the text you want to add. Click the Insert tab, then pick Text Box from the drop-down menu to add more text boxes to your presentation. You can add extra text using this.

5.2 The formatting of the Text

The way things are presented is really important. It would be in your best interest to make your presentation interesting to the people who will be watching it. When you format text, you arrange it by choosing the appropriate font, font size, color, alignment, bullets, and numbering, as well as other formatting options. The following suggestions can help you format your text:

- The size of your text ought to be large enough for your audience while yet being legible. Mark the text you want to change, then choose an attractive font and make it larger. The Font group on the Home tab is where you will find the option to accomplish this.

- Select the text you want to highlight and then pick a color. However, try not to utilize an excessive number of colors on a slide. The Font group on the Home tab is where you'll find the option to choose a color.
- When appropriate, emphasize text by using the Bold, Italics, and Underline formatting options. You may also access these features by going to the Home tab and selecting the Font group.
- There shouldn't be an excessive amount of text in your presentations.
- Before you start to build your presentation, you should first type up all of your material.
- When listing things, choose the "Home" tab and make use of the "Bullets" and "Numbering" options.

5.3 Inserting in PowerPoint

At this point in the process, you will begin incorporating various forms of multimedia into your presentation to create an effective depiction. You will have the option to include new slides, tables, pictures, shapes, icons, smart art, add-ins, links, text boxes, footers, symbols, audio, and video.

Inserting anything into your PowerPoint would comprise the following steps:

- To insert, choose the Insert tab. After that, decide what it is that you want to include.
- There is a slide with a table farther down.
- It is recommended that no more than three visuals be used in each presentation.

5.4 Applying Transitions

Have you ever seen a presentation using PowerPoint that included slide effects? That is what will happen as a result of the transition in your presentation. It determines how the slides in your presentation move. By introducing slide transitions, you may breathe new life into your presentation. To do so, follow these steps:

- Choose the first slide from the slide pane on the left side of your screen before beginning the presentation.
- Simply choose the Transitions tab, then make your selection from the drop-down menu of effect possibilities inside the Transitions group.
- Choose a transition and then choose the second slide to present. Continue in this manner until you reach the very final slide.
- To create a more pleasing impression with your presentation, try using a variety of transitions for the slides.

5.5 Presenting Your Slides

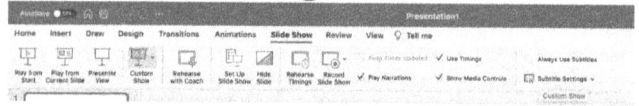

- When you have completed the process of producing your slides and are satisfied that your presentation is complete, the following step is to deliver it to your audience on the day of the presentation. To display a presentation using PowerPoint:
- Launch the file that you want to exhibit to the audience. PowerPoint will open the file for you automatically.
- Establish a connection between your computer and the projector.
- Click the "Slide Show" button and "Play from Start."
- is located on the right-hand side of the PowerPoint interface.
- After the presentation has finished loading, you will be able to continue with your presentation. To go from one slide to the next, use the left and

right arrow buttons on your keyboard. To get out of the slide show and return to the PowerPoint interface, use the Esc key.

Chapter 6: Saving and Printing Your Document

6.1 Saving the File

PowerPoint Online will routinely and automatically save your work for you at regular intervals by default. You also have the option of saving a copy of your work to either your flash drive or a device connected to your computer by carrying out the following steps:

- To save your work, choose "Save as" from the File menu.
- After choosing "Download a Copy," click the Download button that appears in the pop-up window.
- Make the selection to save your file.

6.2 Printing the File

When everything is finished and ready, you can decide that you want a tangible copy of your paper, which you can do by printing it off. Follow the steps outlined below:

- To print the document, go to the "File" menu and pick "Print."
- You will be presented with a dialogue window that has choices to pick how you would want your document to look.
- After selecting the desired quantity of copies to print, click the "print" button.

Book 5 - MICROSOFT ONE NOTE 2022

Introduction

You can view your notes from any device with an internet connection, thanks to Microsoft OneNote's automated syncing and backup features. If you're already using it on your computer, you can simply download the app, log in with the same credentials you use on your computer, and start using it on your phone. As one of the most popular note-taking programs, OneNote makes it easy to collaborate with as many people as you need. Microsoft's carefully crafted apps have superior quality built in, and its improved interface fosters a tighter connection between users and their devices. In addition, Microsoft provides the greatest note-taking software to people all over the globe with its OneNote product. To put it another way, Microsoft OneNote is like an infinitely expandable spreadsheet. OneNote is the ideal organizer since it can replace anything in your desk drawer. By learning how to use this program, you may reduce anxiety by organizing all of your data (notes, graphs, connections, etc.). Make use of Microsoft OneNote and everything it has to offer by following these helpful hints and suggestions. The cutting-edge functionality of the OneNote program will facilitate a wide variety of tasks. For example, you may produce digital notes that you can later arrange and bind, or you can jot down thoughts or write notes that lack a strict format. OneNote isn't only a fantastic digital notepad; it's also a powerful data organizer. This program will save you a lot of time and trouble when it comes to maintaining an orderly database of vital information. You will never have access to a better digital idea processor than this one.

Gathering knowledge may result in chaos if you don't have a system in place for keeping track of your notes, thoughts, lists, and online reading material. The more organized our storage system is, the easier it will be to locate items when we need them. All of your thoughts, no matter what format they are in, may be consolidated into one easily searchable place using the greatest note-taking software. One of the greatest solutions available is Microsoft's OneNote. As it has apps for Android, iOS, macOS, Windows, and the web, it can centralize your data and make it easily accessible from any device.

Chapter 1: How to Get Started

OneNote is a digital note-taking tool developed by Microsoft that is available for free download and may be used to record ideas and thoughts. It allows you to write notes and add material to those notes, and it keeps all of your notes in the cloud. This is helpful if you're probably taking notes in a classroom, if you're at a business meeting, or if you're simply living your regular life, spending time with your family, or planning a trip, and you want to compile all of these thoughts in one location.

1.1 Downloading and Accessing OneNote'

You may be wondering how to get the most out of OneNote and where to find it on your computer. The good news is that OneNote is included with Windows 10, so if you are reading this on a device that runs Windows 10, you already have access to OneNote. How do you get to OneNote? You may do this by going to the search area and typing in "OneNote." When you do this, you will see that OneNote is shown as the item on the list that is the closest match to what you entered. You are now free to proceed and click on it, at which point the OneNote program will launch for you. Unfortunately, if you are using Windows 11, this program will not be pre-installed on your system by default. You can get OneNote by going to the Microsoft Store, which is the only thing you need to do to accomplish this goal.

OneNote is also accessible from inside your web browser, which provides an additional access point. You might start by opening your preferred web browser and go to office.com once it's open. You are going to access OneNote in this manner moving forward. Simply sign in with your Microsoft account after clicking the sign-in button, provided that you already have a Microsoft account. You may also establish a free Microsoft account if you do not already have one by clicking the option labeled "new one" on the Microsoft website. As was mentioned earlier, OneNote saves all of your notes in the cloud. Since they are saved in the cloud, OneNote can synchronize those notes across all of the devices that you are using. Therefore, if you make a note on your phone, it will appear on your computer as soon as it is created. You need to log into OneNote for the syncing to work, and in order to do that, you need a Microsoft account. This account could be one that you use at work or school with Office 365, or it could be one that you use with another Microsoft service such as Outlook or something similar.

1.2   OneNote User Interface

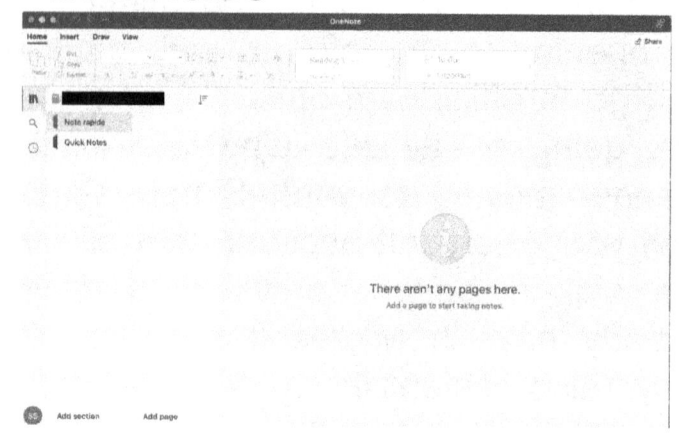

Now that you have Microsoft OneNote installed, the next step is to click on the application, and if you are starting this application for the first time, you will need to sign in with your Microsoft account. If you do not have a Microsoft account, you can click on "Create one," and it will take you to the Microsoft website, where you can create a brand-new account from Microsoft. If you are starting this application for the first time, you will also need to sign in with your Microsoft account. The beauty of this application is that whenever you log into your Microsoft OneNote, it will automatically sync and download all of the notes that you have created in the past; however, if you are using it for the first time, you won't see any notebook, and you will need to create one before you can use it. The appearance of OneNote is the first topic that I'd want to cover concerning this app. You may access a feature referred to as "Show Navigation" by moving your mouse pointer to the upper left-hand corner of the screen. You may now arrange your notes more logically if you go ahead and click on them. Notebooks, sections, and pages make up OneNote's top three most important components, respectively. Pages are organized and kept track of in portions, which are then kept in notebooks. You can see the account for this notebook at the very top of this page. Below that, on the left-hand side of this page, you will see the sections, which include Events, Meetings, Projects, Quick Notes, and Research. If you click on the bar at the top of the screen, you will be able to see all of your notebooks. You may consider this to be a real physical notebook, and you are free to create as many unique notebooks as you choose. You will need to go to the notebook area at the top of the page to create a new notebook. Once you are there, you will be able to see any existing notebooks that you already have, as well as have the ability to search for other notebooks. After that, you'll have a second notebook, which will be shown at the very top of the page, and you can access it by going to the very bottom of the page and clicking the "Add new notebook" button. This will offer you the opportunity to give your notebook a title.

Simply pressing on it, selecting the other notebook, and then pressing again will transport you to the other notebook. This is all that is required to switch between notebooks. You can create what is referred to as Sections inside of a notebook. You can view the pages that are included inside the sections if you look to the right of the part that is under the notebook.

If you want to make a new section inside of this notebook, all you have to do is click the "Add section" button, then give the new part a title.

After that, you may add new pages to the new section by clicking the "Add page" button. When you have an existing page and hit the "Create the page" button, it will add another page for you, and all you have to do to name it is put the title into the box on the right side of the screen.

Your next step is to give this part a new title, which should be Chapter One of your work. Let's say that this unit has two chapters; you can create one more section and call it Chapter Two if you like.

This way, you can easily place these chapters inside this unit, and if you click on the drop-down arrow located under Unit One, then you can see how these chapters are hiding inside this subgroup section. What you are likely to do next is to place these two chapters inside this Unit One; for that, you will simply drag it and drop it inside. Not only are you able to generate subsections and sections, but you also can generate other groups. To do it, just right-click, and choose "New Section" from the menu that appears.

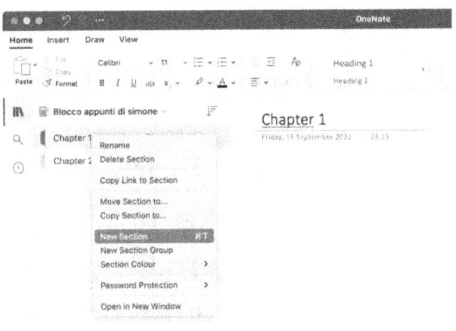

You can see that you have established one Subgroup here and that you have put two parts inside of that Subgroup section. After that, you have built the next Subgroup, and within it, you may have another section. Therefore, if you want to move it, all you have to do to do so easily is drag it upwards or downwards. This can be done at any time. You have the option of making a note on each page. Not only can you text there, but you also have the opportunity to draw, scribble, or make handwritten notes, as well as add pictures, links, and videos. In the next paragraph, we shall go further into these topics. Therefore, you are free to arrange your notebook as thoroughly or as superficially as you see fit; nevertheless, OneNote provides a wealth of options via which you may give your organization a variety of levels, giving you a great deal of control in this regard.

Chapter 2: Saving, Syncing, and Sharing

After you have finished writing in your notebook, there are some steps you may do to guarantee that you do not lose track of your note. This section discusses the measures that you may take to protect your notebooks from being stolen or lost. You have the option of saving, exporting, or sharing your notebook, individual pages, or sections with other people. Let's get going so we can find out more information about how you can accomplish these goals.

2.1 Sharing

Transferring your "Personal" Notebook to your OneDrive account is required if you wish to make it accessible to other users. To do this, launch the "Personal" Notebook, go to the "File" menu, and then scroll down to the "Share" option. Once there, you'll get a message that instructs you to share this notebook; accordingly, you'll need to upload it to OneDrive or another cloud storage service.

SharePoint, when you select it, that file will be saved to OneDrive on your computer. You might also explore it if it isn't mentioned here; alternatively, you could name your notebook and choose "Move notebook" from the menu. After receiving a notification informing you that the notebook is beginning to synchronize to the new location, choose "OK" from the menu. Because you have now placed it in an area where sharing is possible, you will see that all of the sharing choices that were previously unavailable to you are now open to you. This is because you have now put it in a location where sharing was previously unavailable.

2.2 Sharing Using Microsoft OneDrive

Finally, you have the option to move your notebook, which you have already become familiar with because you moved your notebook into OneDrive earlier. It is not required that you constantly publish the whole of the notebook; if you so want, you may choose to share only one page from the notebook instead. If you want to share a page from your notebook, make sure that you have clicked on the page that you want to share, then go up to the Home tab, and you will see that you have an option here to "Email page," as well as a keyboard shortcut of Ctrl + Shift + E. If you want to share a page from your notebook with someone else, follow the steps above. It will open an email in Outlook, attach the contents of the page, and then allow you to choose who you want to share this information with before sending the email. What it does is open an email in Outlook. The user will get an email that contains the name of the notebook as well as a button to open it. If they click on it, it will open up the notebook in the browser, and if that user makes a modification, it will sync that change, and you will see the change in your notebook, along with a small marking showing that it was contributed by the user.

2.3 Synchronizing Data and Saving

When you share notebooks with other people, there is a possibility that more than one person will be able to access and edit the same notebook at the same time. This is an essential fact to keep in mind. Therefore, to guarantee that the data is updated as soon as possible, your notebook has to be synced. To do this, choose the File menu item and then make sure you are in the "Info" section of the menu. You will notice that there is a button over on the right-hand side that allows you to view the sync status. Clicking on this button will display all of the notebooks that you have, along with information about the most recent time they were updated and whether or not they are synchronized. The option to sync automatically whenever there are changes has been pre-selected for you automatically. If you have shared this notebook with five other people, and they are all making changes in this notebook, then any changes that they make are automatically synchronized so that you can see them. This applies only if you have shared this notebook with more than one person. If, on the other hand, you would rather sync manually, you have the option to do so. When you select this option, a check mark will appear on each of these notebooks to indicate that they are not synchronizing at the moment, and you will be able to select the notebook with which you would like to work manually. Therefore, if you click "Sync Now," the icon will transform, and any updates that have been made since the previous sync will be brought up to date. If you have a lot of notebooks stored in this area, there is a single button at the top that says, "Sync All," which will make things much simpler for you.

2.3 Password Protected Sections

When you share your notebooks with others, there is one more thing that you may want to do, and that is to password-protect some areas of the notebook. This stops unauthorized persons from accessing certain parts of your notebook that you don't want other people to view. If you want other people to be able to see everything that is in one section but not everything that is in another section, all you need to do is right-click and select "Password protect This section." After that, click "Set Password," and from this point forward, even if you share this notebook, other people won't be able to see what is on that specific section. To remove protection, right-click the area you want to unprotect, navigate back into "Password protect This Section," select "Remove password," and then enter the previous password.

Chapter 3: Typing and Writing

This chapter will brief you on all the comprehensive knowledge you need to obtain for editing, formatting, and moving the location of your personal section groups.

3.1 Typing

The procedure of typing into OneNote is identical to the process that you would use to text into Word. You can click almost anywhere on the screen and start typing. The usage of the term "anywhere" is, however, the most important aspect of these features. In contrast to Microsoft Word, where your typing is limited by invisible margins and rulers, OneNote allows you to click anywhere on the page and start typing there. When you do this, a little container will be created, but it will become larger as you continue to write. The note, after it has been written, may be picked up and moved to any location on the page, as well as to any portion of the notebook or any other notebook. This is one of the reasons why this container has been provided. When it comes to taking notes, this indicates that you do not need to be aware of the specific location of the note being made with the other ones. After you have completed constructing the notes, you will be able to move them about and match them up with notes that are similar to them.

3.2 Writing

OneNote gives users the option to physically scribble and take notes with their own two hands, in case typing isn't their thing. Now, if you have a tablet that enables you to use a pen on the screen, it is much better than having a tablet that does not have that capability. If not, then it's not a problem at all. Look at the extreme top of the OneNote window; there is a menu labeled "draw," and inside this tab, you will discover choices for adjusting everything from the line thickness to the color of the lines you draw. However, after you are through sketching, OneNote can transcribe the drawing, which is where the app really shines.

3.3 Pictures

The process of importing photographs into OneNote is really straightforward. You will find the option to "Insert Picture" inside the tab labeled "Insert." Simply open the appropriate file by clicking on it here, and everything will be taken care of. The photo can be picked up, moved, and resized in any way that you see fit, just as it can be done with a container.

3.4 Voice Records

One further useful function offered by OneNote is the capability to record sounds. The procedure is really easy to follow; all you have to do is click the "Audio Recording" button, which can be

found in the "Insert" tab. After that, the program will start recording on its own. After that, an audio file of this will be added to the area and page that is appropriate.

3.5 Videos

OneNote is an application that can practically do everything. The objective of the team working on Microsoft is to make the process of compiling and organizing one's notes as straightforward and productive as humanly feasible. Its capability to play videos is perhaps the clearest example of this trait's existence.

3.6 Equations, Tables and Grids

The creation of grids and tables is quite similar to that of a word document. After that, it can be picked up and transported as well. You can then turn this table or grid into an Excel spreadsheet, which is a feature that is exclusive to OneNote and gives it a distinct advantage. After you have done this, you will be able to utilize it in excel. From this location, you will be able to turn the data into any number of graphs and charts that Excel makes possible.

3.7　Webpages and Hyperlinks

OneNote allows users to copy and paste URLs into the app. It is simple and has some degree of success. However, there is a more effective approach to save for later using the information that may be seen on a website. Downloading the add-on is the first step in carrying out this process successfully. After being downloaded, this plug-in ought to automatically install itself onto your taskbar (this varies depending on the web browser that you are using. Now, when you are on the page that you want to add to OneNote, just press the clipper button in the upper right-hand corner of the screen. This will take you to a new menu where you will have the choice of either pasting the whole page into OneNote, manually clipping only a portion of the page, or having the clipper do it for you. If you choose the latter option, you will be redirected away from the original menu. If you are clipping a page that contains a recipe, for instance, the clipper feature will alter the page so that just the recipe and a picture of the dish are shown. After that, the finished product will be downloaded to the notebook that is set as your default, and all you will need to do is move it to the appropriate section and page.

3.8 Personalization

Personalizing your notes and sections is the very last thing you are going to want to accomplish before you go on. Again, this is something that can be done quickly and easily, and it is often done as a method of making one's work more organized and accessible.

Chapter 4: Section Groups

The idea of a section and subsection is being attempted to be realized via the use of section groupings. If you keep your recipes in a notebook and find that you have an excessive number of dessert recipes (is it possible to have an excessive number of dessert recipes?), you might want to reorganize your sections so that you have a section for cakes, another section for pies, and another section for ice cream. You can then place all of those sections under a section group that is dedicated to desserts.

4.1 Choose a Group Section

After you have chosen your notebook, you will need to click on the name of the section group that you desire to pick. Section groups are those multi-tabbed objects that are located to the right of the section tabs. As a side note, you are not able to modify the order in which section groups are presented, so they will always be listed in alphabetical order. If you try to alter the order in which section groups are shown by dragging and dropping a section group, it is possible that what you have really done is shifted a section group such that it is now included inside another section group. This is something to keep in mind as an additional side note. Feel free to inquire about how this was found out.

4.2 Remove One of the Section Groups

You may remove a section group by selecting it with the right mouse button, going to the Delete menu option, and then confirming that you want to transfer the section to the Deleted Notes folder. Click on the History menu, then click on the down arrow to the right of the Notebook Recycle Bin menu item, and finally click on the Notebook Recycle Bin menu item to see your previously deleted notes. Now, right-click the portion you want to restore, and then choose the menu option that says Move or Copy. Finally, tell OneNote where you want it to restore your previously lost area, and it will do so.

WARNING: Deleted section groups will be removed from your account permanently sixty days after you move the section group to the Deleted Notes folder.

4.3 Modify the Name of an Existing Section Group

Simply give the new section a name by right clicking the section group, selecting the "Rename" menu option, and then typing it into the tab that appears. If you want to rename a section group, you can't rename it by double-clicking on the section group as you can with a section.

4.4 Shift One of the Section Groups

You can relocate a section group inside a notebook, either to another notebook or to a section group. You can relocate a section group by right-clicking on it and then selecting the "Move" option from the drop-down menu that appears. After selecting the notebook or section group to which you wish to relocate this section group in the Move Section Group dialogue box, you can then proceed to click the Move button to complete the process. After the section group has been transferred, it will continue to exist in the target notebook (and target section group, if you specified one), but it will no longer exist in the place where it was originally stored. On a mobile device, what can you do with the Section Group that you've created? When you examine the sections included inside the chosen notebook, you will be able to see the section groups along with the parts that are contained within them. You would see the Desserts section group with Cakes and Pies and Ice Cream listed as indented sections beneath the Desserts section group in the example of desserts that was shown before.

4.5 Synchronizing the Section Groups

Long pressing the section group, you want to sync, then pressing the "Sync section group" menu option on the screen that shows your sections is how you do it. Although OneNote will automatically synchronize your notebooks, sections, and section groups in the background when it detects that you've made changes, you can manually force the synchronization of a section group between your device and OneCloud to occur right now if you feel the need to do so for some reason. This is possible because OneNote allows you to manually force the synchronization of a section group between your device and OneCloud.

Book 6 - MICROSOFT ONE DRIVE

Introduction

OneDrive is another web-based cloud storage service that, in addition to letting you save your files and photographs in the cloud, gives you the ability to view those files and photos from any device, regardless of location. Even if you were to misplace your phone or another device on which you had saved your data on OneDrive, you need not worry about losing those files since they would still be accessible to you on OneDrive. Everything there is to know about OneDrive is included in this book. If you have your files saved to OneDrive, even if you decide to upgrade to a new phone or device, you will still be able to access them on your new device. This is because your files will be synced across all of your devices. Through the use of file sharing, you will always be able to stay connected to your relatives and friends when you have OneDrive. It is not necessary to attach huge files to your emails; all you need to do to share your images or files with others is to give them a link in an email that they may click on. Microsoft is among the most successful software titans, and it has been at the forefront of its industry ever since the company was founded. OneDrive is a hard drive in the form of a cloud that you can use to store and share your files, and it is one of the web-based stores that Microsoft operates specifically for the purpose of providing free storage for its customers. Cloud storage, also known as Microsoft OneDrive, is a service that enables users to upload and store digital content such as files, images, and documents online, making it possible for them to access those files from any device and location in the world. The data that is kept in Microsoft OneDrive is kept in the cloud and may be viewed from any device that has the software installed. It makes it less difficult to save data and papers without causing too much anxiety. You will have the opportunity to access all of your important papers, images, and any other items that are connected to your Microsoft OneDrive account from any other device, thanks to the assistance provided by Microsoft OneDrive. It also conducts a lot of work on how to share those photographs or papers with other people, such as friends, family, and co-workers. Your computer, the website, and even your mobile device may all serve as access points for Microsoft OneDrive. It also helps ensure that every file on your computer is kept up to date in the correct manner. If you have shared your OneDrive with other people or devices in the past, those devices and persons will automatically get updated versions of any documents that are being altered or added to OneDrive. The Features of OneDrive, one of the things that set OneDrive apart from other cloud storage options is the fact that users just need an internet connection to access their files and folders stored in the service. It not only saves your files but also makes it possible to instantly share them with any device that is connected to the internet. Using OneDrive, you can do the following:

- You are able to view your files and photographs from a distant location,
- You can modify documents that were originally written on your

desktop computer using your laptop.

- You are encouraged to make your files available to others and to participate in group projects.

Chapter 1: Accessing OneDrive Account

Do you have an email account with Microsoft? – Outlook or Microsoft Live. Consider yourself to be the owner of a OneDrive account if you have any of these capabilities. Easy, isn't it? Launch your web browser, sign in to Office 365 using the email address you use for the service, and then pick OneDrive from the menu on the sidebar to get access to the cloud storage service. This will allow you to access your OneDrive account. After that, you will be sent to a user interface that shows all of the documents that you have saved in other Office 365 applications like Word, Excel, PowerPoint, and others. You also can upload a new file of any kind, which may be done at any time. OneDrive now works better for those who already have a Microsoft account, thanks to improvements made by Microsoft. When you sign up for a Microsoft account, a storage space in OneDrive is immediately added to your account. One unknown thing is whether or if Microsoft is using this method as part of a commercial effort to attract more customers to their cloud storage. Even while the introduction of

OneDrive was a welcome development for the cloud storage system, the vast majority of users are having trouble mastering its interface. When it comes to online storage, the fact that OneDrive performs the same functions as Google Drive and other cloud storage programs is a fascinating development to notice. This is because OneDrive provides you with an entirely web-based location for putting or storing your files. To access your data or files, you will first need to sign in to your Microsoft account. This is similar to the process required by other cloud storage applications.

1.1 Sign up with OneDrive

When you join up with Microsoft OneDrive, there are several steps you must do, including the following:

- To access OneDrive, go to OneDrive.live.com. You will then be presented with the screen shown below, where you will pick "sign up for free."

- Pick the kind of account you want to use. In this scenario, you will have to choose between establishing a personal account and a company account in order to proceed. If you have a business account, the services that are available to you are not free; rather, you must pay a fee to use them.
- Simply enter your email address below. There is a spot for you to input your email address, and if you don't already have one, you have the option to make one for yourself.
- Please enter a new password. After entering your password, you will be prompted to click the "next" button.

Other details at this point, you are asked to provide both your birth date and the country in which you were born. Your email address is awaiting verification. When all of these steps have been completed, a confirmation code will be issued to your phone number or email address so that we can verify that you are the rightful owner of the email or phone number. After that, you will be asked to put in the code so that it may be validated. Confirmation in its final form and the establishment of an account In this section, you will need to demonstrate that you are a human by entering the captcha code accurately. Once you have done so, your account will be established, and you will then be able to upload your files and documents to your account.

1.2 Sign In to Your OneDrive Account

You may sign in to OneDrive in one of two ways: either via the web page or through the application. If you already have the app installed on your device, then you may sign in by following the steps outlined in the section below. In contrast, if the application is not already installed on your computer, you will need to either download it to use it or log in to your account through the website (OneDrive.live.com).

- You will begin by going to the Start menu and typing "OneDrive" into the search bar that appears.

- When the search is complete, you will notice OneDrive among the results; to access it, click on its name. If you already have a OneDrive account, all you need to do is enter the email address that you used to register for the account and then click the "sign in" button.

- After that, go to the next page and input your password there. You will be asked to input an extra code that has been given to either your email address or phone number for correct confirmation of account ownership. This code will be supplied to you if you have already set up some other method of authentication for your Microsoft account.

- To pick the OneDrive folder you desire, you must first follow the guidelines that are provided. If you have previously logged in to this computer, there is a chance that the OneDrive folder was already present on your computer. You have the option of clicking here to utilize this folder or selecting the option to pick a new folder.

Chapter 2: The OneDrive Interface

With a white backdrop, the user interface of OneDrive is really straightforward. Because it is a cloud storage service, OneDrive has a number of features that users may make use of. The following items are helpful tools to have at your disposal while working with your files:

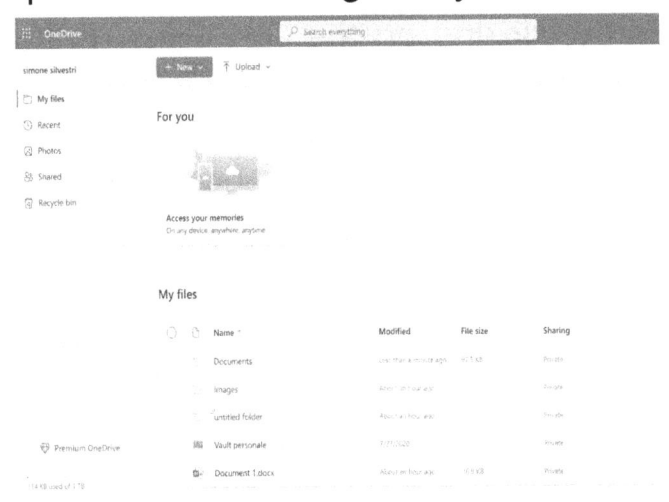

The Toolbar may be found at the very top of the screen in its default position. It may be found at the very top of the screen, just below the title that reads "OneDrive." It has a search box, a new tab, an upload tab, a sort of tab, a view tab, and a tab for the details pane. The Navigation Pane may be found in the far left-hand corner of the screen, just to the left of the space labeled "Files." You can see all of your files by clicking on the "My Files" button, which brings them to the center of the screen. There are other links located underneath the "My Files" heading.

There is a Recent folder, a Photos folder, a Shared folder, and a Recycle bin. Just to the right of the navigation pane is where you'll find the File List Section. This section maintains a record of all of the folders and files that you have submitted. The simplest way to upload files with ease is to just drag them into the area designated for the file list.

You may choose and determine what to do in the File list that is shown. Using the Toolbar, you can search for files, organize them, and upload them. In addition, you can create documents and folders.

2.1 Exploring the OneDrive Window

To get you started, OneDrive provides you with two folders for storing files: Documents and Pictures. In addition, you can create additional folders inside OneDrive. Files may be stored on OneDrive for up to one terabyte or one thousand gigabytes. You can find out how much storage space you have available for saving files by looking in the bottom-left corner of the browser window. Because folders identify how many files they hold, it is possible to determine the total number of files that are contained inside each folder. Simply clicking on the folder's name will allow you to access the folder and examine its contents. Take a look at Figure 1-1 once again and make a mental note of the following file management capabilities that are available in the OneDrive window:

Creating Folder

To create a folder for storing files, click the New button and then choose the Folder option from the drop-down menu. For more information, please refer to the section of this book titled "Creating a folder."

Put your files online

To transfer files from your own computers, such as a desktop or laptop, to OneDrive, click the icon labeled "Upload." Please refer to the latter section of this chapter titled "Uploading Files to a Folder on OneDrive."

Organizing the files and folders in the window

Folders and files may be organized and located with the help of the tools located in the top right corner of the screen. See the section titled "Viewing and Locating Folders in the OneDrive Window" later on in this chapter for more information.

Accessing your Data

To access the primary window for OneDrive, select OneDrive from the menu that appears in the upper-left corner of the screen or select Files from the list of links that appears on the left side of the display.

Chapter 3: Organizing and Managing the Folders

When you create new folders in which to save data, those folders will be saved in OneDrive. OneDrive provides you with two folders for storing files: Documents and Pictures. In addition, you can build your own folders and subfolders inside those folders. On these pages, you will find instructions on how to create folders, navigate inside OneDrive from folder to folder, and perform other folder management operations such as renaming, deleting, and relocating folders.

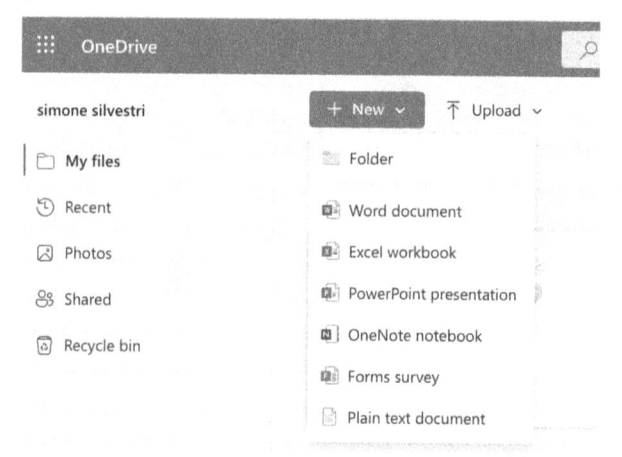

The steps necessary to manage the file list are as follows:

- Creating a Folder or Document in OneDrive
- In OneDrive, you can quickly create new files and folders as needed.
- Click the New tab button located on the Toolbar, and then choose the kind of file you would want to work with from the drop-down option.
- Simply choose "Folder" from the drop-down menu to create a new folder. You are going to see a box. After giving your document a name, click the "Create" button. You will be able to see the folder in the list of files.
- Click on the document you would want to create to initiate the creation of a new document. After that, a fresh tab will be made available for you to work on inside your browser.

3.1 Renaming Documents and Folders in OneDrive

You may choose the folder or document by clicking the little circle icon that appears on the folder or document.

- From the menu located in the Toolbar, choose the Rename option.
- After you have given the file a new name, click the "Save" button.
- Moving and Copying Documents and Folders
- Click the tiny circle icon located on the folder or document that you would want to transfer or copy into another folder. This will allow you to choose the folder or document that you would like to move or copy. If necessary, you may choose more than one folder or document to work with.
- Select "Move to" or "Copy to" from the Toolbar's drop-down menu.

- In the popup window that has shown to your right, choose a different place to search. Then, choose the 'Copy' button.
- Check the integrity of the file once it has been transferred or copied.

3.2 Deleting and Restoring Documents and Folders

When a file or folder is removed, it is moved to the Recycle Bin, which is the place it was most recently located before it was deleted. On the other hand, you can retrieve them from the recycling bin. Take the following actions to accomplish all of these things:

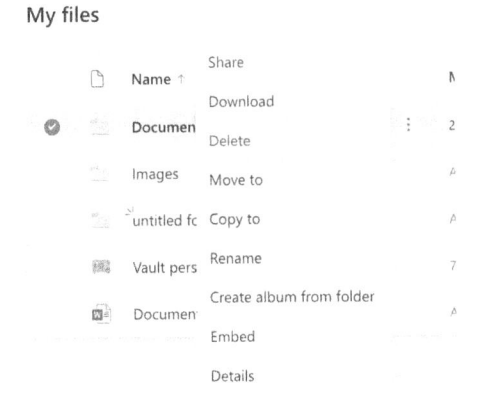

- To remove a Folder or Document from your computer, right-click on the file and then choose "delete" from the context menu that appears.
- To retrieve anything that you have deleted, enter the Recycle bin by clicking the tab labeled "Recycle bin," and then look for the item that you want to restore. After clicking on the item, go to the Toolbar and choose the "Restore" option.
- The recycle bin is where all of the objects that were deleted before they were removed from the system are deleted. In addition, they remain in the recycling bin for roughly a month.
- Simply selecting the "Restore all items" option from the drop-down menu will bring back anything that was previously erased.

3.3 Sharing a Document or Folder in OneDrive

OneDrive gives you the ability to share your papers while yet giving you full control over those documents. Be aware that your folders and documents will remain private unless you want to share them with others. To make your files accessible to others, follow the steps outlined below:

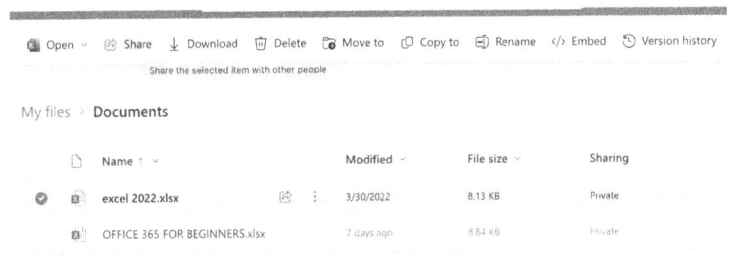

- Click the tiny circle icon that is located on the file that you want to share to choose it as the file that you want to share. Click the "Share" button located in the Toolbar.
- To access further customization choices, go to the popup menu and choose the option that reads, "Anyone who has the link may change."
- Remove the checkmark from the box labeled "Allow editing" to

prohibit your collaborator from making changes to your work. They will not have access to any other features of your document.

- Whenever you are ready, after you are finished, click the "Apply" button.
- In the "To:" field, enter the email addresses of the recipients, and in the "Message" field, type in a note to alert them about your paper. Simply forward your item by clicking the Send button (s).
- Alternatively, you may manually invite individuals by clicking "Copy link" and sending them the URL that you have copied.

3.4 Uploading Files to OneDrive

Following the steps below in your web browser will allow you to upload your files to your OneDrive account:

+ New ⌄   ⤒ Upload ⌄   🔗 Share   ↓ Download   🖼 Create album from folder   </> Embed

My files > Documents

- When you choose the "My files" tab and then click the "Upload" button in the Toolbar, a drop-down menu that displays choices for uploading files and folders will appear. Pick Your Documents.
- A dialogue box will appear, and you will be asked to choose the desired item that you wish to upload from your device to proceed. After clicking "Open," you will need to be patient while it processes.
- After that, you will have the ability to validate your file.

You are now completely aware that OneDrive serves as the repository for all of your files generated by Office 365's many applications. On the other hand, once you have mastered the methods covered in this section of the tutorial, efficiently managing and organizing files and folders in Office 365 ought to be as easy as reciting the alphabet.

Chapter 4: Sharing Your Files with Others

You should make your files available to other people so that they may see, modify, or just view your work. Sharing documents allows many users to work together on a single Office document. From the OneDrive window, you have the option to share either an individual file or a whole folder, which includes all of the files included inside the folder. When you share a file with other people, you are effectively giving them permission to either read your file or view it and make changes to it.

4.1 Sharing the File Directly

You can share a file directly from Word, Excel, or PowerPoint by clicking the Share button, which can be found in the upper-right-hand corner of the screen. This saves you from having to go to the OneDrive window. The Share pane will appear after you have selected OneDrive from the Share window and have then clicked on the Share button. From that location, you may send email invitations to other people to share a file with them or produce a sharing link:

4.2 Email Invitation

In order to send the file to other people through email, you must first enter their email addresses into the Invite People text box. After that, choose either Can Edit or Can View from the drop-down menu to see what kind of editing access the sharer has, and then click the Share button. (If you prefer not to input a sharer's email address directly, you may click the Search the Address Book button instead and then use the Address Book dialogue box to choose the person's name.) (If you prefer not to input a sharer's email address directly, you may click the Search the Address Book button instead and then use the Address Book dialogue box to choose the person's name.)

4.3 Link Generator

Make the file available to others by creating a link to it: Simply click the Get a Sharing Link button (located at the bottom of the Share pane). Then you may create either an edit link or a view-only link by clicking a button. In the last step, choose the link to copy it to the clipboard by clicking the Copy button. You will then be able to copy the link and paste it into an email or a website.

4.4 Email Invitation Process on OneDrive

If you want to share a file (or all of the files in a folder), you may do so by following these steps and sending out an email message with links to the files (see Figure 2-1). One simple click is all the person who receives your email message has to do to read or see the file you attached.

- Make your selection in OneDrive of the file or folder you want to share.
- To share content, click the Share icon.

- On the Toolbar that runs along the top of the screen in OneDrive, you will notice a button labeled Share.
- You are looking at the Share window, which is seen in Figure 2-2.
- To determine whether other users are only able to view the file or edit it as well, select or deselect the Allow Editing option.
- Your decision in this section will influence the access rights that are granted to sharers.
- You have the option of imposing a password as well as a time limit on the files that you plan to share with other people.
- Select email account.
- Within the Share window, there are text fields where one may insert their email address and a message (refer to Figure 2-2)
- Simply enter the email addresses of the individuals with whom you want to share the folder or file.

- To share content, click the Share icon.

To determine which folders and files are shared, you must first switch the Files window over to List view. When they are shared, the word "Shared" will appear in the Sharing column. You may adjust how files and folders are shared, as well as unshared, at any time by returning to the File window. You can access this window at any time.

4.5 Link Generation

To generate a hyperlink that allows you to share a file (or all of the files in a folder), please follow these steps. Once OneDrive has generated the link, you will be able to share it publicly or email it to other people. The file may be seen (or viewed together with editing capabilities) by anybody who hits the link.

- Choose the file or folder you wish to share from the menu that appears when you open OneDrive.

- To share content, click the Share icon.
- You may generate a link to a file or folder using the Share window, which is shown for you to see in Figures 2-3.
- Choose whether you want to allow editing or not.
- Your decision will decide whether other people may access the file as well as change it or whether they can just view it.
- You have the option of putting a password on the files you plan to share as well as setting an expiry date for those files.
- Click the Get a Link button.

This URL was generated by OneDrive. As can be seen in Figure 2-3, it is shown in the Share window.

Simply choose the button labeled Copy. You are free to post the link anywhere you choose at this point, whether it be on a blog, a website, or an email message.

4.6 Accessing Files Shared by Others

To see the names of the folders and files that others have shared with you as well as those that you have shared with others, go to the Shared pane. Clicking the Shared button in the OneDrive navigation pane will take you to the Shared window (located on the left side of the window). You can open files and folders in the Shared Window using the same method that you use to access them in the Files or Recent windows, which is to click on the item. You might also right-click and choose Open from the context-sensitive menu that appears.

Book 7 - MICROSOFT OUTLOOK 2022

Introduction

Do we not all communicate through email? Regardless of the sector in which a person works, sending and receiving emails is consistently ranked among the daily tasks that demand the highest amount of time from its participants. During the course of a typical workday, an individual devotes around 28 % of their time to checking, writing, and replying to emails (as well as looking through them). The majority of the time, emails are not managed correctly, and as a consequence, people find themselves with a cluttered inbox that just seems to become bigger as each week goes by. It is very uncommon for communications to get buried, and users may spend hours separating important and relevant information from less important information. Users of Outlook in Microsoft 365 have access to a multitude of tools that may improve the way they handle email to boost their productivity. However, to get the full advantages of these features, it is necessary to learn how to use them. If you've been looking for ways to make email more productive and less of a time suck, one option you may want to explore is switching to Microsoft Outlook. You do not need to open a new email account; more information on this topic may be found in the content. You can either use it from the list of Microsoft Office Desktop applications or use Outlook on the web, which essentially functions like any other email and is accessible through a web browser either on a PC or mobile and, of course, also has the mobile application that is installable on the app store of each device. It is available in a variety of forms. You can use it either from the list of Microsoft Office Desktop applications or use Outlook on the web. Therefore, the tools that you need to be your most productive and connected self–at home, on the road, and everywhere in between are accessible to you for your emailing life using Microsoft Outlook. These tools are available to you regardless of where you are.

Chapter 1: Outlook Interface

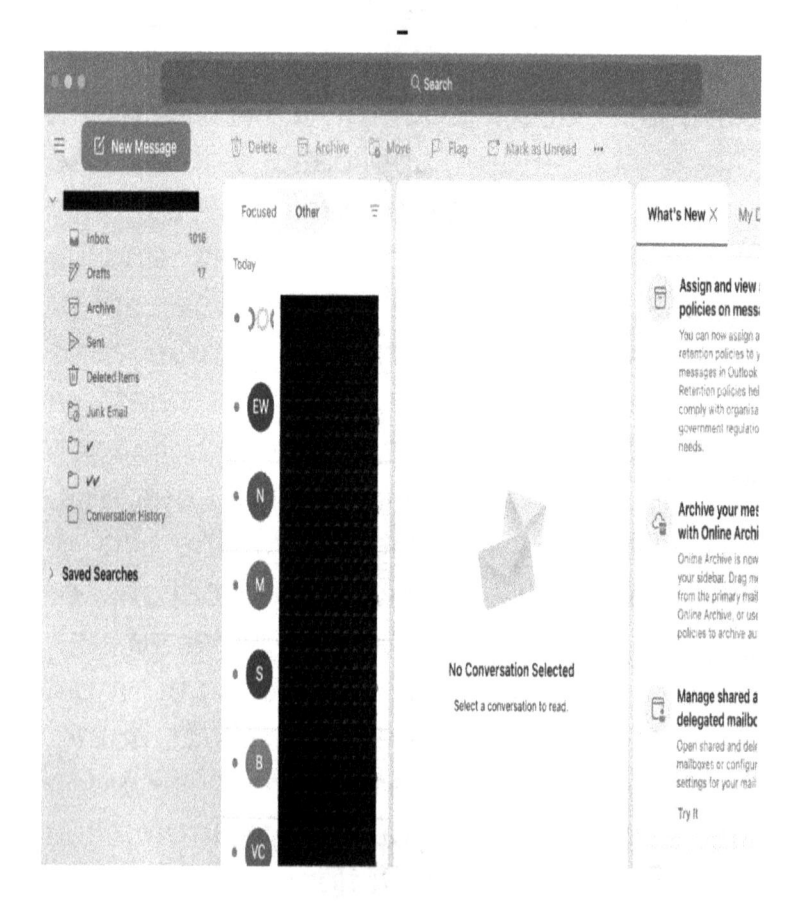

To open Outlook, choose the "Outlook" icon that is located on the left-hand side of the Office 365 user interface. When you look at the UI of Outlook, it might be easy to get disheartened since it seems to be difficult and perplexing. But on the whole, it is a really useful instrument. One interesting aspect of Outlook is that it consists of a large number of distinct regions or parts, each of which has its own individual user interface. These sections are referred to as Mail, Calendar, People, Files, and To Do, respectively. Simply click on one of the icons located at the very bottom of the Outlook user interface to navigate to the area you wish to utilize or interact with. To access additional features, the Outlook user interface has a button with three dots at the bottom. The Navigation pane may be seen on the left-hand side of the screen. It enables you to navigate between the different sections and access the folders in each of them. When you are working in a particular area, the Navigation pane displays the folders that are included inside that area. When you select a folder within the pane, that folder becomes active, and you are then able to work with the functions or items that are contained within it. For instance, under the "Mail" area, you may examine newly arrived messages by clicking on the "Inbox" button.

Chapter 2: Sending and Receiving Emails

Outlook allows you to both send and receive email messages. It gives you a wide range of benefits that may assist you in organizing the whole of your company's business communications. The fact that it works on any device and gives you access to the same dashboard no matter where you are is what gives it its standout quality.

2.1 Sending Mails

Step-by-step instructions on How to Use Outlook to Send email are as follows:

- To start a new message, click the "New Message" button.
- In the "To" field, enter the recipient's email address (s).
- In the "Add a subject" field, enter the message's topic.

- To get started typing, just double-click anywhere in the empty box. The options available above the send button may be used to format your message before sending it.
- To upload an attachment, open the file selection dialogue by clicking the Attach button and then selecting "Browse this computer." Instead, you may choose "Browse cloud destinations" to access your OneDrive files.
- When you are writing, press the "Send" button.

2.2 Receiving Mails

Emails you receive in Outlook will be stored in a folder labeled "Inbox," where you may easily access them. Sending Emails To Multiple Recipients It's not a huge issue at all to send an email to a group of people. Just enter several email addresses in the To area, separating them with commas. You may choose as many recipients as you'd like from your address book at once by clicking the To button; Outlook will take care of adding commas to separate the data for you.

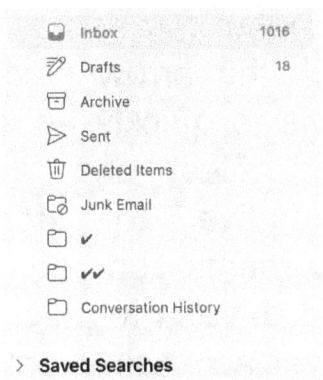

2.3   Attachment-Carrying Email Sending

Go to Home > New Email to send an email with an attachment. Alternatively, you may choose either Reply/Reply All or Forward when responding to an existing email.

Below is a screenshot of the email closing dialogue box:

- If you want to attach a file, you may do so by clicking Attach File and then choosing the appropriate option from the pop-up menu.
- Click the arrow next to Recent Items to quickly access recently used files and images. An alternative to storing these documents on an individual's hard drive is to place them on a server accessible only inside the company's firewall.
- You may attach an email by selecting the menu option Attach Item > Outlook Item.
- By selecting the "Attach Item" menu and then "Business Card," you may add a digital version of

your business card to your message.

- To specify a time frame and other details in a calendar, choose to Attach Item > Calendar.
- Using the Browse Web Locations option - you may choose files from previously visited web locations like your OneDrive, SharePoint sites, or Group Files.

Browse This PC - Initially, you need to select a file from your local computer to upload by clicking the Browse This PC button. You may provide a link to a file stored in OneDrive or SharePoint, or you can attach a copy of the file to your submission. The Permissions for a file in the cloud may be updated using the context menu option to do just that.

Receiving Attachments

When you get an attachment, you should examine it thoroughly to identify whether or not you recognize the sender. Make a judgment on whether or not to open the attachment after seeing it. Select Return to message when you're done.

2.4 Scheduling Message Sending

Automation is essential. If you want your firm to grow in a smart and timely way, you should begin with email. With automation, you may set up messages to send at inconvenient times or when you won't be there to manually initiate the send.

More sales can be made with the aid of automated email marketing since more contacts can be made with prospective clients at the optimal time. Previous research found that compared to manual email marketing, an automated email campaign enjoys a 70.5 percentage point increase in open rates and a 152% increase in click-through rates. This is because targeted emails sent at optimal times to the predetermined audiences have such positive results. Outlook gives you a choice between two options for setting up future email send times. You may opt to postpone the delivery of a single email at the time of sending, or you can set up rules to delay the delivery of all of your outgoing emails by storing them in Outlook for a certain amount of time.

2.5 Scheduling Your Email

After opening the dialogue box to send an email, choose the Options tab, and then click the Delay Delivery option to delay sending the message (this can be found in the More Options group)

- To prevent your package from being delivered before the specified date, go to the Delivery Options menu. Specify the delivery date and time next to the "Do Not Deliver Before" option.
- You may also experiment with the other settings to determine when a message will become unreadable to its intended recipient.
- Choose the Close button. You may now send your email, and it will arrive at its destination at the time you set. The email you just sent will stay in your Outbox until it reaches its destination.
- And if you change your mind and want to send that postponed email/message right away, you may do so by following the steps below:
- Access the computer's Outbox storage area. To send a message at a later time, just choose it from the list.

- Follow the same procedure until you get to the Delivery Choices part.

If you want your email delivered right away, make sure the option labeled "Do Not Deliver Before" is unchecked. Click Close to save your changes and update the delivery date and time, and then uncheck the 'Do Not Deliver Before' box if you want to. If you want to send your email immediately, just click the "Send" button.

2.6 Searching for Emails

There may be occasions when you have an excessive number of emails in your inbox, yet you will need to view a certain message (probably because it contains the useful information you need). Proceed with the steps below:

- Find the search box at the top of the interface for your Outlook program.
- If you cannot recall the name of the sender of the express mail, you are searching for, key in the

phrase or word that was included in the message instead of the sender's name in the search area. This will allow you to discover the express mail you are looking for.

- After the messages have been filtered out, you will be able to find the specific mail that you are searching for.

Chapter 3: Organizing Your Inbox

When learning how to organize emails in Outlook, understanding how to use folders and categories is vital. These are the key tools that you will use in your effort to gain a better handle on the contents of your inbox.

3.1 Folders

Folders in Outlook are accessed by clicking the arrow to the left of your inbox, which is located beneath your email address (this is also called the Navigation Pane). There are two types of folders, which are as follows:

- Default Folders The default folders that come with your Microsoft Outlook application are the typical folders that are used in email. You should be familiar with these folders. The most typical ones are draughts, sent mail, deleted items, trash, spam, and other default folders. Other default folders include trash and spam.

- Personal Folders: Make sure all of your incoming correspondence is well-organized and prioritized by creating additional folders. It is essential to avoid creating an excessive number of folders since doing so might lead you to get confused about which folder to choose.

3.2 How Folders Operate

The user interface for the mail portion of Outlook is composed of a few different components. These tools are designed to assist you in organizing your emails in some way. These components ensure that your mail is organized and sorted properly. Listed below are some of them:

Inbox

The inbox is the location that is largely responsible for storing any new mail that has been received. The instant you launch Outlook, it will immediately begin loading in the background. In addition to the functions of the inbox, it also displays invites for meetings and alerts you if there is a response to one of your messages. The viewing and reading parts make up the outlook interface, respectively. The contents of the inbox are shown in the watching area, while those that are chosen in the viewing section are displayed in the reading section.

Sent Items

The folder referred to as Items That Have Been Sent in Outlook stores copies of items that you have previously sent using Outlook. The primary purpose of it is to store the stuff that you have sent.

Drafts

It is a folder that stores copies of emails that you are drafting but have not yet sent. Additionally, it saves copies of the messages that you have not yet sent, which is useful when you don't want to send them right away but do want to send them at a later time. After returning to the folder, you will be able to access the draught and continue producing the document.

The Deleted Items folder

Items from other folders that you have removed from Outlook and moved to this folder are preserved here.

Junk Emails

Outlook classifies an email as junk mail if it were sent to you by someone the program does not recognize or that you do not feel comfortable trusting.

Archive

The Archive folder in Outlook stores preserved messages that you may choose to hide from other users. Your most critical emails will be stored securely in this folder.

Notes

The Notes function may be used to jot down personal information and to keep track of ongoing tasks. Using the Notes feature of Outlook, you may save vital information that you do not want to lose and that you do not want to be forgotten. From this location, you'll be able to see the notes that you've generated. You can go to your Notes by choosing "Note" in the bar that runs across the top of the screen.

3.2 Categories

The use of categories makes it easy to color code your communications. It is entirely up to you whether or not you, for instance, designate the color red to indicate communications that demand urgent attention, the color green to indicate messages that require prompt action, the color purple to indicate meetings, and so on. There are a variety of applications for using color coding. You will want to devise a plan that is tailored to your specific needs. When your inbox is organized using color-coded categories, it is much simpler to have an option that lets you go through your messages and decide what to do with each one with just a quick look.

Chapter 4: Other Features in Outlook

In addition to these capabilities, we will be talking about the Calendar, People, Files, and To Do lists.

4.1 Calendar

The Calendar view allows you to organize and keep track of the events that you are currently participating in. A connection has been made between the calendar and the Outlook app. You can get to it by clicking on the "Calendar" icon that is located at the very bottom of the Outlook user interface. By utilizing the calendar interface, you will have access to the Calendar grid as well as the Folder pane: You can see the calendar for the current month as well as the next month on the folder pane, and you can also navigate through the months of the year. The calendar grid will display the dates that you have chosen on the calendar. The month view displays the whole of the month, with the day that is now actively being highlighted. To add a new event to your calendar, go to the top left corner of the user interface and click on the icon that says, "New event." The next step is to add a description, followed by a reminder, the date, and the time. When you are finished, click the Save button.

4.2 People

The Contacts view allows you to manage the record of people you communicate with regularly. The "People" icon, which is located at the very bottom of the Outlook user interface, can be used to gain access to it. The reading pane displays the information of any communication, the folder pane displays the folders that you have created, and the contact page displays the contacts that you have created. These three primary components can be found, from left to right, in the Contacts view.

4.3 Files

This is where your attachments, or the files that you have attached to emails that you have sent and received, are stored. The 'Files' icon, which is located at the very bottom of the Outlook user interface, may be used to get access to it. It is possible to copy, relocate, or store files in a new place on either OneDrive or the local computer.

4.4 Remote Accessibility

You may monitor your emails from any location, and your progress is synchronized across all of the devices you use, as has previously been stated but bears repeating for emphasis: When everything is in its proper location, synchronization functions perfectly even if your internet connection can produce synchronization problems, problems with your firewall, and other similar problems. Note that if you begin using Outlook on a new device while still using an older email address, it will take some time for your previous messages to get synchronized on the new device. You don't need to step in. The synchronization, on the other hand, will function without your intervention; all you need is a connection to the internet that is operational. You are good to go, and you may use it anywhere, whether on your mobile device, your desktop computer, or both.

Book 8 - MICROSOFT TEAMS

Introduction

Microsoft Teams is a powerful tool that takes the process of interacting and talking with other members of your team to a whole new level. Using Microsoft Teams, it is possible to collaborate from any location, regardless of the number of people doing so—two, three, or even ten thousand. The notion of working remotely is gaining popularity among teams located all over the globe. Microsoft's goal is to maintain connectivity amongst teams even when members are located in various physical places. To this end, Microsoft Teams is being made accessible to as many people as possible. There is no need to go somewhere else since teams allow you to have conversations, meetings, phone calls, study sessions, and cooperate all in the same place. Continue reading for some useful advice on working from home, and don't forget to sign up for Teams so you can start using it for free right now. The 'future of workplaces' is brought to life by Microsoft Teams, which lives up to its name. Teams are designed to facilitate collaborative work amongst co-workers via the exchange of files, participation in chats, and even participation in voice and video conversations. Microsoft Teams is designed to accommodate the ever-evolving needs of today's contemporary workplace, in contrast to the document libraries and task lists that are part of SharePoint, which represent more or less permanent data repositories. It's possible that during the course of a year, you'll find yourself playing for many different teams. You may find yourself engaging in many channels while being part of the same team. This book explains the concepts of teams and channels. It demonstrates how to inform colleagues when you are busy or available for collaborations, how to start a discussion with them, as well as how to have a private talk with them. You may get up and running more quickly by using Microsoft Teams for your video conferencing and communication needs. This will assist ensure that your needs are met. Examine the specifics of this component to have an understanding of how it may most effectively serve your team.

Chapter 1: Accessing and Getting Started with Microsoft Teams

As was seen in earlier chapters of this book's tour of Microsoft 365, you may access teams by using the Microsoft 365 App Launcher. You may also get access to Teams by going to https://www.microsoft.com/en-ww/microsoft-teams/ and logging in there. As was just said, Microsoft Teams are also downloadable via the various app stores for mobile devices. As is customary, a single account guarantees that you can monitor all of your activity from any device, irrespective of where you happen to be. You may also get Teams on your own computer by going to the homepage of Microsoft Teams and selecting the button that says, "Download Teams."

Chapter 2: The Formation of Teams and the Administration of Channels

To get down to the nitty-gritty of the situation, all of these things have to be put into practice to enjoy all of the advantages that have previously been mentioned. When using Microsoft Teams, a "Team" refers to a group of people that collaborate toward the achievement of a certain objective; in many cases, the whole of a company will be included in a single Team. In the meanwhile, Channels function similarly to subgroups that are a part of the organization. They are divided into groups, with each group being committed to a certain department, project, or piece of work. Imagine, for the sake of this illustration, that Teams is a corporation and Channels is the sales division of that same organization. Therefore, channels are made after a team has already been established.

The following procedures may be followed to set up channels and teams:

2.1 Create a Team

Launch the Microsoft Teams program, and from the choices accessible at the bottom of the Teams sidebar on the left, pick "Join or create a team." In the new screen that has just been shown, click the button labeled "Create a team." On the screen that follows, you will be given a choice between selecting:

- Establish a brand-new team from the ground up; this will be a fresh group of players.
- Make a new team by cloning an existing group or team in Office 365.

If your team was previously using Office 365 before migrating to Teams, you might already have groups that can be imported by utilizing the option to "Create from..." If your team was already using Office 365 before moving to Teams, you might already have groups that can be imported. If this is not the case, you may go through with the plan to "Build a team from scratch." After that, you should choose the individuals that will make up the team. Consider the following factors while making your decision, keeping in mind how you want the structure and organization of your platform to look:

Private

Choose this option for situations in which a group needs to consist of no more than a select few individuals, as an example.

Public

The public is the optimal setting for groups that are constantly reorganizing their membership rosters.

The Org-Wide

The Org-Wide option is the one you should go with if you want to host your whole organization on the platform as a single 'team' and use channels to divide up the work and ensure that everyone is on the same page when it comes to communication.

- After settling on the composition of the group that you want to put together, the next step is to give it a name.
- After providing an appropriate team name, such as 'Sales' or 'Social Media,' click the 'Create' button located in the bottom right corner of the screen to finish creating the team.
- After you have finished creating your new team, your new team will immediately appear on the new page.
- You may add members to the team by either clicking on the three dots that are located next to the Team name from anywhere in the team app or by using the 'Add additional people'

option that is located on the homepage of the Teams app. Simply type in the names of the people whose participation you want to be required for the group.

- You might offer them guest access instead, using their email address as both a login and a password, if they are considered to be "guests," which refers to individuals who are not affiliated with your organization.

2.2 Make a Channel

After a team has been created, it is time to start including channels in the group that has been created. In order to collaborate effectively as a team, you need to have channels. When Microsoft Teams is initially started up, it will immediately create a general channel that will be accessible to all members of the team. It is possible to add more channels. To begin, go to the team you would want to add a new channel to and click the menu option that reads "Create additional channel." On the homepage of the Team website is a link that reads "Create more channels." You will be able to choose a name for the channel from the menu that appears, provide a description for the channel, and change the privacy settings so that either all team members or only a select few team members can view the information. All of these options will be available in the pop-up window that appears. After you have done customizing the channel, you can begin the process of creating it by clicking the 'Add' button in the configuration window.

2.3 Defining Your Status

When you indicate your status, it is much simpler for your co-workers to determine whether or not they may communicate with you. Make it a practice to update your status so that other members of the team always know whether or not they can contact you and how to do so. In order to manage your status inside Teams, follow these steps:

- Open your user menu. The menu may be accessed by looking in the top-right-hand corner of the screen. When you open it, a drop-down menu appears before you.
- When the status option, which is the first choice on the menu, is selected, a drop-down menu with other status choices will appear.
- Pick one of the options: Available, Busy, or another one.

Consider the scenario in which you need to determine if a co-worker is free, occupied, or absent. Start entering the name of your co-worker in the Search box located at the very top of the screen once you have moved your mouse there. Your colleague's name needs to be included on a list that may be dropped down. Simply click on the name of the person you are conversing with to get to that person's page.

Chapter 3: Everything You Need to Know About Conversations

Conversations aren't a mystery if you're familiar with social media platforms like Facebook or LinkedIn. You can contribute to a discussion by posting, commenting on the postings made by others, and liking a post. Conversations amongst employees are about more than just talking about a certain subject. Dialogue may also serve as an essential record of a subject, its history, or its context. Newcomers to a channel are able to catch up on the latest developments in a project by simply browsing the dialogue that is taking place in that channel. Co-workers can evaluate a discussion to determine how far along a project is, discover what questions have been asked in the past, and investigate the history of a project to see how it has developed over time. On these pages, you'll find instructions on how to save a discussion as a bookmark, add a conversation to your favorites, start new conversations, and respond to existing ones.

3.1 Liking and Bookmarking Conversations

To like a discussion and add it to your bookmarks in Teams, follow these steps:

- Proceed to a channel's Conversations page when you're ready.
- When you enter a channel, the Conversations page is the first page that you see.
- Move your mouse pointer over one of the posts.

You will see the following three buttons:

More options

Opens a drop-down list with choices for flagging a post as unopened, copying a hyperlink to the post to the Clipboard, or accessing the post in Immersive Reader. Clicking the More Options button opens the drop-down list. Within Microsoft Teams, there is a unique view called Immersive Reader that makes it simpler to read through lengthy chats.

Save the message

This function will save the message so that you may examine it at a later time. To access posts that have been saved, visit the user menu and choose Saved from the list of options.

Like the message

This user likes the post. Everyone on the team may see the posts that you liked.

You have numerous options at your disposal when interacting with channel postings, including the ability to like them and save them for later use.

3.2 Beginning a conversation

To get a discussion started, just follow these steps:

- Proceed to a channel's Conversations page when you're ready.
- Please provide your message in the space provided.
- Tools for inputting emojis, hyperlinks, and other goodies are located underneath the text field in the document. In order to

inform a colleague about the discussion, you want to begin, write the at symbol (@) followed by the colleague's name into the text box. This will alert the colleague about the conversation you intend to begin.

You can attach the discussion to other channels in addition to alerting the other participants. Followed by the at symbol (@), type the name of the channel you want to join. You may send the message by pressing Enter or the Send button. Every member of the team can hear and see what you are saying.

3.3 Responding to a conversation

To publish a response in response to a chat, follow these steps:

- Proceed to a channel's Conversations page when you're ready.
- Click the Reply button that is located in the message to which you wish to respond.

- After you have finished typing your message, either hit the Enter key or select the Send button.

3.4 Having a Confidential Conversation with a Colleague

There are instances in which some individuals in a team should not voice their inquiries, criticisms, or worries. There are instances when the content of a communication is best kept between two persons or a small group of carefully chosen employees. Make sure your interactions stay under wraps by using the Chat function. When using Teams, you should never make a remark that you wouldn't want your manager or IT administrator to see. Even a chat message that is only supposed to be intended for a small group of people cannot be considered really private. Administrators of Teams can audit and access all material included inside a Teams workspace. This is done for purposes of both security and regulatory compliance. Follow these instructions to begin a private conversation with one or two individuals of your choice and to take part in the conversation:

- To start a new conversation, choose the New Chat button located on the navigation bar that runs along the top of the screen.

- You may access the New Chat option by looking to the left of the Search box for the symbol that resembles a pen and paper.
- A list of recent users will show whenever you start a new conversation or participate in an existing one on the Chat page. If you wish to take up where you left off with a prior chat, you may choose a name to do so.
- After entering your message, make sure you hit Enter.
- You are presented with a Chat window.

When someone wishes to talk with you, a notice will appear in the bottom-right corner of the screen. Simply clicking on this notice will bring up the Chat window, where you can then begin conversing. To send a message, type it into the box labeled "Type a New Message," then either press Enter or click the Send button To bring in other participants to a conversation, choose the "Add People" option. The location of this button may be found in the top-right-hand corner of the display.

Chapter 4: Functioning of Searches and Filters

There are times when it is beneficial to reduce the amount of "noise" and focus on exploring stuff that is relevant to your professional interests. You may filter the activity of the team to view just the things that are relevant to you by beginning on the Activity page. You also can run detailed searches. The Activity tab provides a centralized location for quickly locating anything relevant to you, including channels, discussions, chats, files, and so on.

4.1 Filtering Your Activity Feed

The activity feed compiles all of the possible activities that may be carried out inside the channels in which you are now participating. The activity feed, which is where you may discover mentions, responses, and other alerts, is a common place for individuals to check first thing in the morning when they arrive at work. Using the following techniques, you may filter your activity feed so that it focuses on the information you require:

- To access the Activity tab, choose it from the Navigation bar.
- If it isn't already chosen, the Feed option should be picked from the Activity selection.

The activity selection may be found at the very top of the window that displays the activities. The picker provides the following two options:

- Feed which displays all of the posts and mentions that you have received.
- My Activity displays the posts that you have started.

Simply choose an alternative from the list that appears when you click the Filter button. As illustrated in Figure 4-7, you can filter your activity stream using a variety of different criteria. Adjust the settings on the activity feed of the team so that you are only shown the events that are relevant to you.

4.2 Trying to Locate Some Content / Searching

How exactly do you go about locating the file that your boss casually referenced a week ago? Or do you remember the name of the movie that a co-worker recommended to you in a one-on-one conversation around three months ago? Performing a search in Teams for a certain post, message, or file may be done as follows:

- Put the cursor in the box labeled Search or Type a Command from any page in Teams and start typing.
- This text box may be seen running horizontally across the

top of the screen.

- You can either type in a search term or enter a command starting with a forward slash (/) followed by a search term.

A search word may be "reports" or "Sales department reports," for example. You could also just use "reports." You may combine a search for a person, channel, group, or file with a specific action by using the forward-slash command. When you input the forward-slash (/), a list of instructions will display in a drop-down menu. Select a command, then type a search word, and then hit enter. For instance, choose /chat and then send Mark a message via chat. Press Enter.

The results of the search are shown on three tabs: Messages, People, and Files, respectively. Choose a tab to narrow down your search and get more specific results. I hope that you are successful in finding what you are looking for.

Chapter 5: Participating in Meetings with Colleagues

Meetings may be held in one of two ways using Teams. You and a colleague have the option of participating in a meeting via the use of audio or video technology, or you can go back to the tried-and-true method of setting up a face-to-face appointment on a certain day and hour.

5.1 Holding a conference (Audio or Video)

To successfully host a video or audio meeting, proceed with the following steps:

- Find the person you are hoping to speak with.
- Carry out a global search or look for the person's user symbol in the chat history or Chat window on your device.
- When you open a person's user card, you may access it by clicking on the person's name.
- A person's name and a picture of that individual are both printed on the card.
- Click the button labeled "Video Call" or "Audio Call" located on the user card.
- The recipient of your call will be notified that you have placed a call to them. At this point,

the individual has the option of either declining or accepting the call.

- Simply pressing a button on the user card will get the call started.

You may conduct the chat or end it by using the buttons that are located at the bottom of the Call window:

Webcam

Switches the webcam on/off

Microphone

Controls microphone's muting/unmuting

Sharing

Let other participants view your screen

More Options

Provides an additional menu for putting the call on hold, transferring, and other options

Hang Up

Terminates the ongoing call

5.2 Setting up a Meeting and Sending out Invitations to Participants

To arrange a face-to-face meeting with a fellow worker, please proceed as follows:

- In the navigation bar, choose the Meetings tab to get started.
- Simply click the Meeting Scheduling button.
- Using the New Meeting box, provide a summary of the gathering and ask others to join you there.
- Give the gathering a title, decide where it will take place, specify when it will take place, and invite the appropriate employees.
- To see your schedule, click the icon.
- Your calendar has been updated to reflect the meeting.
- Colleagues are notified in the form of a message that a meeting is being requested. Invitees may respond to the communication by clicking one of three buttons—Accept, Tentative, or Decline—that are included in the message. When a meeting request is approved, it is added to the calendar straight away.

Chapter 6: Add Further Application to Your Teams

It's possible that you'll need to add other applications like Planner, To-Do, and Sway to make use of them inside the Microsoft Teams app; however, this is a simple process as long as the app in question is included in your subscription. Launch Teams, then use the search bar at the bottom left to find and add your preferred application; keep in mind that it must be compatible with your membership. The screen that displays the app's description will appear after you have selected the app that you desire. Spend a little time going over all of the different subsections (e.g., Tabs, Messages, Personal app.) This section will outline the capabilities of the application, as well as how and where it will be accessible inside Teams, allowing you to utilize it as is or modify it as you see fit. After that, choose the Add button, and at that point, your app will be accessible for use inside the app that your team uses.

6.1 Linking up Streams with Teams

Microsoft Stream is a corporate video solution that provides you with the capacity to develop and securely distribute videos inside your own organization. Stream is easy to use in many aspects. You and your other employees can work together on videos by utilizing applications that you are already acquainted with, like SharePoint, Teams, and Yammer, in addition to a web browser. Microsoft Stream incorporates enterprise search, complete with smart search capabilities and intelligent searching, as a standard feature. Because of this, it is easy to generate and distribute content, as well as to obtain the information you want at the time you require it. Microsoft Stream is the replacement for Office 365 Video, and your Office 365 Video accounts will be converted to Microsoft Stream. If you have previously used Office 365 Video, you should be aware that Microsoft Stream is the successor to Office 365 Video. If you are worried about the safety of uploading your videos to a service that is located outside of your firewall but would still want some assistance,

Microsoft Stream can provide it. Enterprise-level protection is provided for Microsoft Stream, just as it is for the other components of the Office 365 suite. Because your users have signed in, they have access to videos, and the permission levels on particular films may be modified to restrict access to some users while allowing others to view. When utilizing Microsoft Stream, you can choose who you want to share content with, whether it be a select group of individuals on your team or the whole of your company. Using Microsoft Stream, everybody in your company can take part in and benefit from video collaboration, and the platform ensures that every video is kept secure. Microsoft Stream also helps organize video material into channels and categories, making it simpler to find what you're looking for when you need it.

6.2 Organize Using Channels and Groups

Channels are an excellent tool for classifying and organizing the available content. You may bookmark videos or rapidly follow a channel to make sure you don't miss any new ones that are uploaded. If you are a subscriber, this part of the homepage will enable you to see any new videos that have been uploaded to a channel and will make it simple to locate the channel that you follow. Click the Following button to stop following a channel that you are no longer interested in. However, Stream's Groups are modeled around Office 365 Groups in both appearance and functionality. When you create a group in Stream, it will automatically build a new Office 365 Group. This group will have its own email address, calendar, and site that can be accessed throughout Office 365. If your company already makes use of Office 365 Groups in other places, such as Microsoft Teams, SharePoint, Yammer, or Planner, you can immediately begin utilizing them in Stream. While channels are primarily used for organizing videos into sections and authors, groups are developed specifically to impose restrictions on video permissions. To a greater extent, groups take measures to limit the audience for their videos.

6.3 The Option of Creating Live Events

It is usually recommended by Microsoft that you configure your video, community, and user rights at least twenty-four hours before the event to have the best possible experience. This may be shown by, among other things, the addition of users, the modification of video permissions, or the transition of a community from private to public status. It may take up to two hours for some changes to take effect in Microsoft Stream, Microsoft Teams, and Microsoft Yammer. Testing may be done, and adjustments can be made, if required, after at least twenty-four hours have passed.

Chapter 7: Using MS Teams Has Numerous Real-World Benefits

The end-to-end capabilities of Microsoft Teams meetings can do a great deal to help in the elimination of irritation and inefficiency by integrating everything you need for every meeting into one location, thereby making it easier to manage. This is accomplished by integrating everything you need for every meeting into a single location. You may use the chat function to add things to the agenda, documents that need to be read in advance, as well as other topics that will be discussed during the meetings that you are preparing for. Since of this, you won't have to go through your emails to find the meeting notes because everything is consolidated into one location. When the meeting starts, you may use video to keep everyone focused on the topic at hand by turning on the camera, blurring the background to eliminate distractions, and showing live subtitles throughout the discussion. This can be accomplished by using a combination of these techniques. Utilizing the digital whiteboard that is included with the program allows you to not only work together in real-time on papers created with Office 365 but also generate new ideas immediately.

7.1 Teams Offer In-group Storage Space

In addition to the capacity to have conversations, Teams also offers a repository that can be used to store documents, spreadsheets, presentations, and other types of media assets. In addition to storing these files, you also can collaborate in real-time with other users on any of these files. Teams provide you with the ability to work on projects in a single area using Office apps like Word, Excel, and PowerPoint. You could create a team, give it a name, explain what it does, and then ask other individuals to join your group. You may easily include someone by using the at symbol in a conversation or by requesting them to join a team. Both of these methods will achieve the same result. Microsoft Teams is also accessible in its entirety on mobile devices, with all of the capabilities that are available on the desktop version. Therefore, your place of work may always be with you, regardless of whether or not you are near a computer.

7.2 Boost Your Teamwork with Microsoft Teams

Users of Microsoft Teams can work together on projects as "digital teams" within the Microsoft Teams platform, which enables users to take their collaboration to the next level. You may be able to encourage a more open dialogue among your various teams by using channel chats. You may also be able to hold online 'meetings' and have speedy access to the applications you require to carry out your work. Workgroups can cooperate more successfully with the help of Microsoft Teams, which is unified software that brings together all of the tools that need to be productive. This software then presents workgroups with a single, unified app. To summarize, cooperation may be elevated to a higher level, made more robust and effective, more possibilities explored, and less work done if Microsoft Teams is used. Microsoft Teams consolidates everything you need into a single, convenient location. Instead, then reading emails and phone conversations individually, arranging meetings, and then meeting on another app (such as Zoom or Google Meet), everything can be brought together in one app, allowing for easy and seamless communication.

7.3 Back-ups Everything in a Centralized Location

Because each member of your team receives a significant quantity of emails, it is quite simple for information to be lost in the shuffle and disappear into the sea of messages. Microsoft Teams can aid in the resolution of this issue by giving your workers a centralized area in which they can cooperate. The conversations that take place in a workplace that is based on chatting are archived in a single area, making it easy to search for them and assess what was said. It gives you the ability to store files, notes, and other information directly next to the chat window, making it accessible to any member of the team at any time. You might also review the chat sessions that were made throughout the audio or video talks to get a deeper comprehension of the events that took place during the meeting. You are free to quickly express both your creativity and your opinions. In-person meetings, phone chats, dialogues in the corridor, and brainstorming sessions are all fantastic ways to generate innovative ideas, but they are not always convenient for everyone who is participating. You are required to hold off until everyone has arrived at the same area. In addition, there is no straightforward approach to conveying and developing one's ideas when inspiration strikes at an unusually early or late hour compared to the norm. Teams make it possible for a more impromptu approach to be taken toward the process of collaborative creativity, which is helpful. The chat box is available for your team members to use when they have questions or comments for you and want to share them. It is easy to initiate a meeting on the spur of the moment using any combination of text, video, or audio communication, or even all three of these approaches simultaneously. To move things along, all you have to do is check the availability of the individuals involved, contact them, and ask when they will be available. When working in groups, you can move at the speed of the ideas being generated. All in one location.

7.4 Facilitation of Collaborative Work

In today's fast-paced environment, it is not uncommon for several people to collaborate on the production of a single piece of work, such as a paper, spreadsheet, or presentation, from its inception until its conclusion. The terrible truth is that communicating information with other individuals via the use of email is not the most effective method for people to collaborate on a project. It is quite easy to get side-tracked and lose track of the primary focus. During the process of translation, a great deal of subtlety is lost. Another disadvantage of the method is the amount of time that is lost attempting to establish which version is the most up-to-date. Teams provide the opportunity to interact in real-time using familiar Office apps on your desktop or through the internet, regardless of where you are physically situated. This may be done either locally on your computer or remotely via the internet. Using its co-authoring function, which provides you with the piece of mind that comes from knowing that everyone engaged is on the same page, you may be able to write a final draught more quickly. This would allow you to save time. It is feasible for a large group of individuals to work in tandem on the same document at the same time. You are promptly notified of any changes made by other users, which makes it easy to coordinate adjustments made by several users. When you open a document that has been shared with you, you will see that any changes that have been made are flagged. This eliminates the need to transmit documents back and forth through email, which may lead to challenges with versioning as well as a waste of important work time. Your team will be able to work together on the deliverables that are so vital to the success of your business when you use the co-authoring feature.

7.5 Maintain Contact Even When You Are on the Go

It may be challenging to maintain crucial team relationships when workers are dispersed around the workplace, whether they are working from home, on an airplane, at a client location, or just dashing between meetings. When utilizing a number of different gadgets simultaneously, it is far more challenging to focus on a single task. They will be able to relax a little bit more in their daily life now that they have the unified collaboration center to help them out.

Book 9 - MICROSOFT ACCESS 2022

Introduction

Even among those who have heard of the app, the majority of individuals have no clue what it does or how it may be used, and this is true even among those who are acquainted with it. The first version of Microsoft was introduced in1990, and with it came a variety of packages, some of which are no longer in use while others are. The database organization and analysis software, known as Microsoft Access, was originally made available to the public in the year 1992. It was extensively utilized and enjoyed for a considerable amount of time, but when other software programs were developed that virtually performed the same activities, it faced a great deal of competition. The widespread use of this tool, on the other hand, skyrocketed once Microsoft included it as a standard component of their Office suite in the year 1995. Therefore, one could say that Microsoft Access has been coasting on the success of Microsoft itself, which is not necessarily a negative thing considering that the tool itself is capable of performing a great deal of functionality that is essential in this day and age.

Since that time, the application has been included in the Microsoft Office evolutionary pipeline, which means that it has to undergo comprehensive testing at the same time as the development of various other Office components. Because of this, Access is currently in the situation that it is now in. To put it another way, Microsoft Access is being used in the process of developing a relational database management system. After you have entered your data, Microsoft Access will organize them and then analyze them in the most relational manner that is feasible. You just need to provide the information, and Access will handle everything else. When you have a large number of records to enter into a database, Access is an especially helpful tool. If you use Microsoft Access to sort this, you won't have to worry about making any mistakes, and you'll also find that your job goes much more quickly. Additionally, working with and navigating through this database won't be difficult.

Microsoft Access was developed by Microsoft and is used as a tool. It is used as a DBMS. It was first distributed to the public in November 2022, and since then, several revised versions have been made available, the most recent of which is the Microsoft Access, 2022 edition.

The next chapter will talk about the many different things you can do by utilizing Microsoft Access, such as establishing large databases, creating databases with several tables, communicating with SharePoint, and learning how to use Microsoft Access once the program has been installed.

Chapter 1: Database Terms You Need to Know

It is simple to get confused by database terminology. Fold back the bottom corner of this page to avoid yourself from tripping, and come back to this section if any of the following database words are unclear to you

1.1 Cell

A "cell" is a spot in a database table where one item of data may be entered at a time. In a database table, cells are created at the points of intersection between fields and records.

1.2 Database

A database is a methodical approach to arranging information in such a way that it can be accessed and altered with relative ease.

1.3 Table

A table in a database is a collection of data entries that are organized into clearly defined fields or categories. The vast majority of relational databases consist of many tables.

1.4 Dynaset

The results of a search for data in a database are referred to as a dynaset. (This phrase is a shortened form of the phrase

dynamic set.) It is important to note that a dynaset is not the same thing as a dinosaur.

1.5 Field

A field is a single section of information included inside a database table. In a traditional table, the columns are analogous to what is known as "fields."

1.6 Filtering

Finding entries inside a database table that all have the same or nearly the same value for a field is an example of filtering. When searching a database, filtering is a method that is more convenient but not as complicated as other methods.

1.7 Foreign Key Field

The field that, in a relationship between two database tables, exists on the "many" sides of a one-to-many connection. This field is referred to as the "foreign key field." The field that contains the main key is located on the "one" side.

1.8 Form

A form is an area that has text boxes and drop-down lists and functions similarly to a dialogue box. It is used to insert entries into a database table.

1.9 Module

The term "module" refers to a process written in Visual Basic whose function is to carry out a certain action in Access.

1.10 Object

An object is an umbrella word that refers to the tables, queries, forms, and reports that you may build and open after beginning in the Navigation pane.

1.11 Primary Key Field

In a database table, the primary key field is the field in which one-of-a-kind, one-of-a-kind data is kept. To query more than one database table at the same time, the databases must contain primary key fields.

1.12 Query

An inquiry that is sent to a database to extract information from it is called a query. A single database table, many database tables, or even other queries themselves might be the subject of a query.

1.13 Record

A record is a complete set of information on a single person or item that has been entered into a database table. A record may be thought of as being analogous to a row in a traditional table.

1.14 A relational database

It is a kind of database software that stores data in more than one database table, creates connections between the columns, and allows users to run queries and generate reports by compiling data from many tables. The database that Microsoft Access uses is a relational one. A flat-file database is one that only supports a single table in its structure.

1.15 Report

Information extracted from a database and organized in a report in such a manner that it is simple to read and comprehend. Printing and distributing reports are the intended purpose of reports.

1.16 Sort

To sort is to reorganize the entries in a database table such that they appear in alphabetical, numerical, or chronological order in one field. This may be accomplished by using a sorting algorithm.

Chapter 2: Tables, Queries, Forms, and Other Objects

One of the challenges of being familiar with a database application is that you can't just dive right in, which is also the fundamental reason why so many people find databases to be intimidating. To be able to utilize database terminology, you need to have an understanding of how data is stored in a database and how it is extracted. You need to be familiar with objects, which is the generic name that Access uses for database tables, queries, forms, and everything else that goes into making a database a database. These sections provide a crash course in databases to assist you in getting started. They describe the many items that comprise a database, such as the tables, queries, forms, and reports that are there. Put on your seatbelt and buckle up. You are prepared to make your first database if you successfully finish the crash course without experiencing any technical difficulties.

2.1 Store Information in Data Tables

Database tables, such as the one shown in Figure1-1, are used to store the information that is included in databases. When creating a table for a database, you should be sure to include one column for each kind of information that you want to retain on file. In a database, fields serve the same purpose that columns do in a table. When you initially begin the process of creating a database table, one of your first responsibilities will be to name the fields and notify Access of the kind of data you want to keep in each column. Figure 1-1 shows a database table that may be used to store information about employees. ID, First Name, Last Name, Email Address, Business Phone, Company, Job Title, and Home Phone are the eight fields that are included in this section.

2.2 Forms for Inputting Data

After the fields in the database table have been created, you may begin inputting entries into the table. A record is a written account that details all of the information that pertains to one person or object. Even though entries may be entered directly into a database table, using a form to input a record is the most straightforward method. Forms, which are very similar to dialogue boxes, allow users to input information by selecting options from drop-down menus and typing into text fields, as illustrated in Figure 1-2. When filling out a form, it is quite easy to understand what type of information has to be entered into each section.

2.3 The Terms "Macros" and "Modules."

This mini book does not go into detail about macros and modules, yet both of those things are database objects. A macro is an abbreviated form of a collection of instructions. You are able to store macros for Access tasks such as running queries and performing other Access operations. A set of Visual Basic procedures and declarations that are used to carry out activities in Access is referred to as a module.

2.4 Putting Together a Database File

Access provides users with two distinct options for creating a new database file. You have the option of starting from scratch or using a template to guide you through the process. When you use a template, a portion of the work is already completed for you. The query builder, forms, and reports are all pre-configured and included with the template. On the other hand, templates are intended for users who are already familiar with working with Access databases. You need to be familiar with modifying an already existing database in order to make use of a template. Determine the location on your computer where the database file will be kept before you begin creating the file itself. Access is unique among Office products in that immediately after creating a new database file; you are required to save it and give it a name.

2.5 Making a New Database Using a Blank File

If you want to build a database file from scratch, follow these instructions:

- Choose New from the File menu's drop-down menu.
- The New window will now open.
- Simply choose the icon labeled "Blank Desktop Database."
- You will be prompted to choose the folder in which your new database will be kept when the corresponding dialogue box opens.
- Simply choose it by clicking the button.
- You are presented with the dialogue box labeled File New Database.
- Choose the directory in which you want to save the database file, give it a name in the text box labeled "File Name," and then click the "OK" button.
- Simply choose the option labeled Create.
- A blank table and the Navigation pane are shown here. The section titled "Finding Your Way around the Navigation Pane" is located

further on in this chapter and describes what the purpose of this page is. I strongly advise that you make haste to get to that location.

2.6 Aiding from Pre-existing Templates

Templates may be quite useful, but only if the user can customize them as described above. Access provides preconfigured databases that may be used for a variety of purposes, including managing assets, maintaining inventory, scheduling resources, and more. Unexpectedly, the only method to determine whether or not one of the templates is worth using is to go through the pain of creating a database based on a template, opening the database file, and looking at it.

To generate a database file using a template, create a database using these steps:

- Choose New from the File menu's drop-down menu.

- The New window should now be visible.
- To obtain a template from Microsoft's online repository, either select a template to download or use the Search box.
- Applications, as opposed to databases, are represented by templates with a globe icon. Access programs are made to work in conjunction with various web browsers.
- Simply choose it by clicking the button.
- The dialogue box labeled File New Database is brought up.
- Choose the directory in which you want to save the database file, give it a name in the text box labeled "File Name," and then click the "OK" button.
- Simply choose the option labeled Create.
- A blank table and the Navigation pane are shown here. Continue reading to learn how to go about

the Navigation pane and where everything is located.

2.7 Navigating Through Different Sections

When you open the majority of database files, the Navigation pane seen in Figure 1-5 is the very first item that you see on the screen. This is where you should begin conducting any work in Access; it is the launchpad. From this point, you may choose an item to work with and get to work right away (that awful phrase again!). When you create a table, query, or other objects, it will automatically be placed in the Navigation pane so that you may access it later.

Finding and choosing items using the Navigation pane is seen in Figure 1-5.

The following are abbreviated instructions for doing the following, among other things, in the Navigation pane:

Selecting a Category of Object

Choose a group from the Object Type drop-down list located at the top of the Navigation pane, such as Tables, Queries, Forms, Reports, etc., or pick All Access Objects to see all of the groups at once, as shown in Figure 1-5.

Generating a New Object

Go to the Create tab and choose the kind of item you want to make from the drop-down menu there. If you want to base a new form or report on a table or query, you may do so by clicking on a table or query in the Navigation pane while you are building a new form or report.

Opening an object

Perform one of the following actions to open a database table, query, form, or report: You can either right-click it and select Open from the shortcut menu, or you can double-click it and then press the Enter key on your keyboard.

Opening an object in the Design view

In the Design view, you will be tasked with the responsibility of constructing database tables, forms, and queries. If there is a need to modify the structure of an object, right-click the object and then select Design View from the shortcut menu.

Finding objects

You can find whatever you're looking for by using the search bar that's located at the very top of the navigation pane.

Initiating and Terminating the Navigation Pane

To open and close the Navigation pane, press the F11 key on your keyboard or click the Shutter Bar Open/Close button that is located in the upper-right-hand corner of the Navigation pane. This will cause the pane to shrink and move out of the way. You can also change the size of this pane by clicking the very right edge and then dragging the mouse in either direction.

Chapter 3: Creating a Database Table

Creating the tables and inputting the data is the first step in setting up a database. This is also the most significant aspect of the process. After you have entered the data, you will have access to your database and will be able to query it for information about the items and people that your database monitors. This book's previous chapters explain what database tables are and how to create an outstanding example of one. The Create tab is where one should begin the process of creating a table in a database. Access allows users to build database tables in one of three different methods, each of which I will discuss in further depth in the following pages:

- Start from scratch when creating the table in the database: You are responsible for entering data and formatting each field individually.

- Utilize a model as a guide by doing so: Obtain a table that has prefabricated fields already built. If you have a solid understanding of Access and can alter database tables and table columns, you should proceed in this manner.

- Import the database table from another database: If you can recycle data that has previously been recorded in a database table inside another Access database, you may save a significant amount of time by using this method.

3.1 Making up a Database Table from the Ground

Creating a table from scratch requires first making the table itself, and then inputting the data for each field individually. Following the opening of a database file, you may construct a database table from scratch by following the procedures below:

- Navigate to the tab labeled Create.
- To create a table, use the Table Design button.

The window labeled "Design" will now appear. You will now input fields for your database table using this screen. I despise the fact that I have to act like a bureaucrat at City Hall who gives everyone the runaround, but I just can't help myself. For information on how to input data into the fields of a database table, go to the section of this book titled "Entering and Altering Table Fields."

To save your changes, use the Save option located in the Quick Access toolbar. A dialogue window labeled Save As will open. After giving your table a name that accurately describes its contents, choose the OK button. When you go back to the Navigation pane, you will see that the name of the table that you created is shown there. If you don't trust me, you can check out the names of the tables in your database by clicking on the Tables group.

3.2 Developing a Database Table Using a Model Template

If you are familiar with Access and know how to make changes to database tables, one of the worst things you could do would be to build a database table by using a template. Access provides the following four kinds of templates: Users, Contacts (which can be used to store contact addresses and phone numbers), Issues (which can be used to prioritize issues), Tasks (which can be used to monitor projects, their progress, and when they are due), and Tasks (for storing email addresses). Access not only generates tables, but it also generates ready-made queries, forms, and reports to go along with the tables it generates. After you have created a table using a template, you will have the option to delete any unnecessary fields. Eliminating fields is almost usually the simpler option compared to adding new ones. When using a template to generate a table (and the corresponding queries, forms, and reports), the following procedures should be followed:

- If any items are left open, be sure you close them all.

- You may close an item by either clicking the Close button on the object's tab or right-clicking the tab and selecting Close from the shortcut menu.
- Click the Application Parts button that is located under the Create tab.
- There is a drop-down list that displays choices for constructing tables and forms. (You may find the tables in the section labeled "Quick Start.")
- Make your selection from Users, Contacts, Issues, or Tasks.
- A dialogue box will appear if your database already contains other tables, and it will ask you whether or not you want to make a relationship between the table you're creating and another one.
- Choose the button labeled "There Is No Relationship," and then click the Create button.

If you want to create these relationships right now and you have the means to do so, select an option other than There Is No Relationship, select a table from the drop-down list, and then click the Next button to choose which field to forge the relationship with. If you want to create these relationships right now, select an option other than There Is No Relationship. Select Design View from amongst the options of numerous drop-down menu that appears when you right-click the name of the table in the Navigation pane (or just click the Design View button in the lower-right corner of the screen). When you are in Design view, you will be able to see the names of the fields that are included inside the table. Check out the section under "Entering and Altering Table Fields" further down in this chapter if the table already has fields that you do not need or if you want to modify the names of the fields.

3.3 Introducing a Table Across from Another Database

The process of inserting entries into a database table is one of the most laborious tasks possible. If the records you need were already recorded somewhere else, then you have one less thing to worry about. To get a database table from one Access database and import it into another, follow these steps:

3.4 Navigate to the Tab Labeled External Data

You may add a new data source by clicking the New Data Source button, selecting From database from the drop-down list, and then selecting Access from the sub list.

- A dialogue window labeled Get External Data – Access Database is brought up.
- After selecting the Access database that contains the table you need using the Browse button

in the File Open dialogue box, proceed to click the Open button.

- You are brought back to the dialogue box labeled Get External Data – Access Database.

- Click the OK button after selecting the first-choice button, which will allow you to import tables, queries, forms, reports, macros, and modules into the existing database.

- The Import Objects dialogue box appears before you, just as it does in Figure 2-1.

- Choose the database table you wish to work with from the Tables tab.

- You may import more than one database table by selecting the tables you want to import one by one or by selecting all of the tables at once using the Select All option.

- You can import the structure of a table, which includes the field names and formats of the table, but not the data that is included inside the table. To do this, open the Import Objects dialogue box, click the Options button, and then in the section labeled "Import Tables," pick the options button labeled "Definition Only" (refer to Figure 2-1).

- Select the OK button.

Chapter 4: Uploading the Data in Datasheet View

The process of entering data in the Datasheet view is quite similar to the process of entering data in a traditional table. A datasheet, much like a table, is formatted with columns and rows. Rows are used to insert records, and each column is used to represent a different field. Those who use the Datasheet view enjoy the flexibility of being able to see a dozen records all at once. These pages include instructions on how to modify a datasheet's look and how to insert data into a datasheet for users who prefer the Datasheet view. When you double-click the names of database tables in the Navigation pane, the tables load in the Datasheet view by default. If, on the other hand, you find yourself staring at a table while in Design view, you may switch to Datasheet View by clicking the button in the status bar or using the View command on the Home tab.

4.1 Entering Data

When you are in Datasheet view, the bottom of the window will inform you of the total number of records that have been inserted into the database table as well as the record that the cursor is now in. To begin entering a new record, you must first navigate to a new row that is vacant and then begin entering the data. Choose one of the following options to generate a new row:

- Click the New button that is located on the Home tab.
- To create a new record from scratch, use the datasheet's navigation buttons to choose the New (Blank) Record option. These buttons may be found in the far-left corner of the Datasheet view window at the bottom right corner.
- Scroll down until you reach the bottom of the window displaying the datasheet, then start entering the row that has an asterisk (*) next to it.
- To proceed, press CTRL. (The plus key).

The row selector will show you the record you are currently working with by displaying a pencil icon next to it. You may go from one field to another by clicking on a field, using the Tab key, or pressing Enter on your keyboard.

4.2 Modifying the Overall Datasheet's Appearance

Try playing about with the look of the datasheet to see if you can make it a bit less crowded and cumbersome to use. Access provides some helpful shortcuts that may be used to do just that:

Rearrange the columns

Columns may be rearranged by clicking the column's name at the top of the datasheet and dragging it to the left or right. This will allow you to relocate a column to a new spot.

Resize the Columns

When you want to resize a column, move the cursor between the column names at the top of the datasheet. When you see an arrow with two heads, click it and start dragging it to the desired size. Move the cursor between the column names and double-click the mouse until you see the arrow with two heads. This will cause the column to expand until it is just broad enough to accommodate its widest entry.

Varying Fonts

The Calibri 11-point font is selected as the default for a datasheet; however, the Home tab has instructions that allow you to change the typeface as well as the size of the font. You may find these commands in the category labeled "Text Formatting."

Varying the Gridlines

Changing the appearance of gridlines requires opening the drop-down menu that is located on the Gridlines button of the Home tab. From this menu, you can choose several choices to modify the number of gridlines as well as their thickness.

Alternate row colors

On the Home tab, click the button labeled "Alternate Row Color," then open the drop-down list that appears, and choose a color to use for alternating rows on the datasheet.

Chapter 5: The Art of Data Presentation in a Report

The information included in a database table or query may be shown in a report in the most aesthetically pleasing manner. Even those who have a hypersensitivity to databases can tolerate database content that is included in a report. The reports are simple to read and comprehend. They give the facts in a condensed form so that it is easier for you and others to comprehend. This short chapter will walk you through the steps of creating reports, opening them, and making changes to them.

5.1 Setting Together a Report

Access is equipped with a wide variety of complex tools that can be used to create your own report. These tools allow you to design the layout of the pages in a variety of ways and position data fields in a variety of locations throughout the page. Developing a report is the kind of job that should absolutely be done with the assistance of a wizard. By eschewing the complicated report-creation tools and instead delegating the task to the wizard, you can save yourself a great deal of hassle while simultaneously producing reports that have an elegant appearance.

5.2 Viewing/Opening the Report

If you have worked with Access for any length of time at all, you are familiar with the procedure for opening a file that is referred to as an object. To open a report, proceed with the following steps:

- Choose the Reports group from the drop-down menu in the Navigation pane.

- You are presented with the names of the reports that you have prepared.

- You may open a report by either double-clicking its name or right-clicking it and selecting Open from the shortcut menu.

In the Report view, the report should show. Go to the Home page and select the Refresh All option to bring an existing report up to date so that it incorporates newly contributed data.

5.3 Modifications Made to a Report (Tweaking)

As I said at the beginning of this book, Access provides a wide variety of sophisticated tools that may be used to alter the format and presentation of a report. You are more than welcome to take these instruments into your own hands and go to work on them if you are brave and you have a lot of spare time on your hands. Right-clicking a report inside the Reports group of the Navigation pane will bring up a shortcut menu from which you can choose Layout View. The Layout view is shown for your report. In this view, you may modify the look of your report by utilizing the tools that are found on the tabs labeled Report Layout Tools. I will walk you through the process of generating a report via the Report Wizard so that you won't have to confront this intimidating display. If you follow these methods, you will be able to alter the look of a report while viewing it in Layout view without going too bothered. Altering your report's layout may be accomplished by clicking the Stacked or Tabular button located on the Arrange tab of the Report Layout Tools or clicking the Gridlines button and selecting an alternative from the drop-down list that appears after clicking that button. Incorporating page numbers To include page numbers into the report, go to the (Report Layout Tools) Design tab and select the option labeled "Page Numbers." A box labeled "Page Numbers" appears. You may pick the Page N option button to show simply the page number, or you can select the Page N of M option button to display both the page number and the total number of pages in the report (for example, "Page 2 of 4"). Choose from the available choices for Position and Alignment to specify where on the page number should be placed. To change the margins, go to the Page Setup tab of the Report Layout Tools, click the Margins button, and then choose Normal, Wide, or Narrow from the drop-down list.

5.4 Report Tweaking Made Easy

Transferring a report to Microsoft Word, where it may be edited, is one of the simplest ways to make adjustments to a report. To convert an Access report into a document that can be opened in Word, follow these steps:

- If you are thinking about exporting your data to Word, go to the External Data tab, click the More button in the Export group, and then choose Word from the drop-down list.
- The Export - RTF File dialogue box appears before you.
- After selecting a location to save the Word document using the Browse button and the File Save dialogue box, you can then click the Save button to finalize the process.
- Select Open the Destination File After the Export Operation Is Complete from the drop-down menu in the Export - RTF File dialogue box.

- To continue, choose the OK button.

Your report from Access will be imported into Word in a minute. The file is in RTF, which stands for "rich text format."

You may save it as a Word document by going to the File tab, selecting Save As, clicking the Browse button, and then opening the Save As Type drop-down list in the Save As dialogue box and selecting Word Document. The file will then be saved.

Conclusion

Productivity is almost all that matters in today's world. Because you have so much to do, and I'm not exaggerating when I say this, you should utilize a tool that can assist you in leading a more productive life, and Microsoft 365 is, without a doubt, one of such things.

It's possible that we've already seen how much it may cost us when we get caught up in the web of work and get overwhelmed by the amount of work that has to be done. On the other hand, if we utilize the tools that are included in this Microsoft 365 package to help us be more productive and efficient in our job, we may not come into situations like these as often.

This book has previously gone over how to browse the interface, so it shouldn't be too difficult to find out how to utilize Office 365 after you've gotten the hang of navigating it. Office 365 comes with a variety of programs, each of which is straightforward to use. The most significant productivity programs, including OneDrive, Word, Excel, and PowerPoint, have all been covered in this book, which has both simplified and broken down their functionality.

However, you always have the option to go over and over again to deal with the confusing sections. When you do this, you will comprehend things more quickly, and once you do, they will always be a part of you.

You can keep track of everything you do by syncing across all of your devices, and you can take notes whenever you need to, using any device that is available to you. You can also find your notes whenever you want, even if you are using one of your other devices, which enables you to plan like a pro efficiently.

Discuss effective methods that may assist you in working with others as well. This user guide has put you on the correct road to beginning to profit from it, and it can only grow better the more you use it. Increasing your productivity with Microsoft 365 is possible no matter where you are, whether it is at home, at work, or school.

Finally, thanks to the exceptional qualities of Office 365, you may access all of your files from any location so long as you have an active internet connection. After logging into the Office 365 interface all that is required of you is to continue working on either newly created documents or ones that have already been created. Working in this manner is referred to as working "on the fly."